A DOG FOR ALL SEASONS

The Labrador Retriever

Edited by Joe Arnette

Orginal dust-jacket artwork
by Dann Jacobus

CAMDEN, MAINE

ISBN 0-89272-563-X
Library of Congress Control Number: 2002112332
Printed at Versa Press Inc., East Peoria, Illinois

2   4   5   3   1

Countrysport Press
P.O. Box 679
Camden, ME 04843

For book orders and catalog information, call 800-685-7962, or visit
www.countrysportpress.com

CONTENTS

ACKNOWLEDGMENTS

INTRODUCTION
    Joe Arnette, Editor

1   *The Labrador Retriever—Who Is He?*   **1**
    Richard A. Wolters

2   *Backwater's Morning Harpsichord*   **7**
    Bob Butz

3   *A Dog's Best Friend*   **13**
    Robert F. Jones

4   *Upland Passage*   **23**
    Robert F. Jones

5   *Changing Needs*   **31**
    Joe Arnette

6   *Retriever Tribulations*   **37**
    Bobby George, Jr.

7   *A Dog Named Bernie*   **51**
    Geoffrey Norman

8   *Knuckleheads and Wild Ringnecks*   **65**
    E. Donnall Thomas, Jr.

9   *The Cartway of Time*   **75**
    Ted Nelson Lundrigan

10   *The Retriever Game*   **83**
    Boyd Gibbons

11 *King Buck*   **93**
     Richard A. Wolters

12 *The Labrador Letter*   **103**
     Joe Arnette

13 *Tales from The Dark Side*   **109**
     Michael McIntosh

14 *The Marsh*   **119**
     Jim Spencer

15 *One*   **133**
     Gene Hill

16 *Just Me and Daisey*   **143**
     Pete McLain

17 *Matters of the Heart*   **153**
     Chris Cornell

18 *Yellow Dog*   **161**
     E. Donnall Thomas, Jr.

19 *Obligations*   **177**
     Steve Wright

20 *The Problem with Holly*   **185**
     Tom Huggler

21 *Gypsy*   **191**
     Jerry Gibbs

22 *An Ordinary Morning*   **201**
     Joe Arnette

EPILOGUE   **207**
     Gene Hill

ACKNOWLEDGMENTS

By definition, a diverse anthology like *A Dog For All Seasons* cannot be a one-person enterprise. Above all else, such a volume requires the cooperation of the authors who originally produced each piece to allow their property to be reprinted, and to be altered in keeping with a publisher's editorial policy and the needs of an individual book. In that vein, this collection owes its existence to the seventeen authors who contributed their work—either one piece or several—to the book. I offer each of them, or in a few cases, their legal representatives, my sincere gratitude.

My thanks to Chris Cornell, editor at Countrysport Press, for suggesting that I compile this anthology, for guiding me through certain pieces of the aggravating minutiae and legal realities of "permission in publishing," and for applying the final, critical coat of editorial polish to this collection.

To my wife, Kathy, as always, I offer apologies for my rough edges; and my thanks for tolerating those occasional bursts of grouchiness and pique when, for whatever reason, this anthology bogged down.

That leaves the Labs, the point of it all.

Undeniably, the Labrador retriever deserves a book of its own, though it is probably impossible to celebrate, in one volume, all of the diverse virtues of this splendid breed. To be sure, there will always be an angle, an event, a bit of uniquely Lab behavior, a singular individual, or a first-rate story that merits inclusion in a book, but slips through the editorial cracks. That said, this book is a tribute to the Labrador retriever as a breed, and to each individual Lab, of whatever ilk, that is a part of that marvelous whole.

Finally, aside from what is in this book, let me personally acknowledge my admiration for all of the black, yellow, and chocolate Labradors—my own and those of others—that have graced my life for so many years and provided me with so many fine moments.

INTRODUCTION
By Joe Arnette

As dog breeds go, the Labrador retriever does not have an especially long and illustrious career history; at least, not in the sense of the distinctive, versatile, much-loved, yeoman gun dog/companion dog that we know today. In fact, within the overall scope of American dog ownership, the immense popularity of the Labrador is a recent phenomenon.

By way of example, the breed was not officially recognized by the American Kennel Club until 1917, when the organization registered its first Lab. It took another fourteen years—December 21, 1931—for the small but influential Labrador Retriever Club to organize this country's initial licensed retriever field trial. And a good many additional years passed before Labs were finally acknowledged as more than weekend retrievers at estate shoots or trial dogs for a few wealthy sportsmen and began their spread into the broader population of American bird hunters.

However, in that relatively short span of time—from the beginning of its dispersal among the general public to today—the Labrador retriever has managed to capture the collective heart of both hunting and non-hunting Americans like no other breed in existence.

Consider that in 1964, the American Kennel Club registered

the comparatively meager number of just over 10,000 Labradors. A mere thirty-six years later, in 2000, the number of Labs registered had exploded to more than 170,000 individuals. Since 1991, the Labrador retriever has topped the list of the most popular dogs—of all 148 currently recognized breeds—in the United States. And, whether gun dog or non-gun dog, the competition isn't even close. American Kennel Club registrations for the year 2000 place the Labrador almost three-to-one ahead of the all-breed runner-up—another retriever, the golden. Labradors outstrip all pointing dog AKC registrations by more than four-to-one; and by a good two-to-one if we add in other registering organizations. Labs also account for well over half of all AKC sporting breed registrations.

Granted, some of the Labrador retriever's surge in popularity and decade-long retention of top honors is a measure of current canine chic: For better or worse, Labradors are in vogue. By no means, though, can a fashionable trend account for the Lab's singular success in the home and field. More to the point, as I see it, is the breed's unrivaled talent for fulfilling the multiple roles of loyal companion, dependable guardian, tolerant babysitter, indefatigable playmate, willing Sunday-afternoon-couch-potato, and, perhaps most of all, of superlative, all-around upland bird and waterfowl hunter.

I think it is safe to say that very few other breeds—if any—can come close to performing all of these human-dictated duties. I think it is equally certain that if there is a competitor in the "Dog for all Seasons" title chase, no other breed can give everything they have to offer quite as naturally, effectively, and lovingly as the Labrador retriever.

These wonderful dogs do indeed have a knack for stealing your heart, along with a skill at getting inside your head. When I think about the many Labradors that, in one way or another, have been part of my life, it strikes me that if, as we all want to believe, there are dogs born to devote themselves to doing what we want them to do—for no other reason than we want them to do it—those dogs must be Labs. Let me tell you about one of them; a Labrador retriever that typifies what the breed is truly all about.

• • •

Almost from the moment I lifted the eight-week-old bundle of black from the security of his littermates, this dog spent his life focused on me. He was constantly attuned to my moods and body language. He seemed aware of what I wanted from him and, in some mysterious way, often anticipated what he thought I might want from him. I didn't fully train this Lab, at least in the standard meaning of finishing a non-slip or flushing retriever. I realized— though not as quickly as I should have—that life with him involved more demonstration than repetitive drill, more guidance than impersonal instruction. I showed him what to do, helped him understand my intentions and, as much as anything else, tried to match his commitment to the full-time job of friend, companion, and hunter. He performed those duties to the fullest with an understated simplicity that was easy to take for granted, and, even, to overlook. As is so common with the breed, my years with this Labrador were an effortless joy.

I'm ashamed to admit this, but in that stretch of my life I hunted everything that flew, ran, hopped, and swam. If an animal was edible or, if I am honest about it, just there, I was after it. I didn't need a more complex reason for pursuit than a passing rumor of availability. And when I was hunting, which accounted for the bulk of my time, so was this particular Lab.

During his life, he patterned, sprinted, dog-paddled, and low-crawled from sea level to tree line. He hunted a hodgepodge of game birds and varmints, and retrieved an outrageous assortment of prey. He worked in near-blizzards and on the fringes of hurricanes; he was with me—on foot, snowshoes, and horseback—in the iron-cold of high-country winters and the moistureless blaze of deserts. He followed my frequently obsessive, and occasionally foolish, pursuits without hesitation or a hitch in his gait. He did everything that I asked of him, and he got every job done—whether normal, oddball or, as much as not, hair-raising—along with chores that I didn't ask of him.

To be sure, living with a Labrador whose every glance asks, *What can I do for you?*, demands a large measure of awareness and responsibility and, on occasion, tolerance and humor. Consider, for example, one particular June morning.

I was on a sharp bend of a western river, bow-hunting breeding carp (as I said, for no reason other than the carp were there and so was I) that had moved into their spawning flats along the water's edge. As usual, my Lab was with me for company. I had tossed down a light jacket on a piece of high ground up from the river, told him to lie down on it and stay there. Then I got on with what was, in retrospect, the pointless business of arrowing carp.

Fifteen minutes and two fish later, I took a break and walked to where I had left the dog. He was gone, but to the side of my jacket, where he was supposed to be lying, was a small pile of carp. I looked round the bend and saw him standing in a foot of water working the splashing fish like a bear in a salmon river. He grabbed another, trotted back and dropped the carp on his pile, then laid down at the exact spot where I had first put him. He looked at me with a curious expression as close to existential as a dog can get—somewhere between uncertain chagrin and contented accomplishment. He had disobeyed my command to stay where he was, which rarely happened, but at the same time delivered the fish that, after watching me, he had apparently decided were more important to me than perfect obedience.

In the same perceptive-Labrador vein, there was the evening that this Lab and I, along with several of my bird-shooting partners, had stopped at a friend's house after a late-day pheasant hunt. This friend was noted for a constant supply of beer kept iced-down in a washtub in his mud room. A sizable mound of cans lay crushed on the floor when we started arguing about who should get up for more. Without really thinking about what I was doing, I stroked my Lab's head, then pointed to the mud room and told him that it was his turn to get a round. He stood up, stared at me for a moment, glanced at the empties, then moved off toward the mud room.

One of my friends muttered, "He's just wandering where you pointed. He won't do it." I was as stunned as the rest of the group when he came back into the living room, sat in front of me, and deposited a cold can of beer in my hand. That was his first beverage delivery, but to my never-ending delight, it wasn't his last. On the downside, popping a snap-top seemed beyond his power. But, given that he was a Lab, I am confident he would have mastered the job in time.

Lest you think that all this Labrador did was perform odd-ball chores like snatching carp and fetching beer, I must tell you that he was a fine upland flushing dog and an unquenchable waterfowl retriever. During his active years, he found, flushed, and fetched a greater number of a greater variety of game than most dogs would confront in three lifetimes. And he did his work not by way of superior, one-of-a-kind talent, but through breed savvy meshed with an astonishing ability to focus on and interpret what he perceived as my every want. From an admittedly biased and self-serving—and very human—perspective, I came to view his goal in life as a complete devotion to my happiness, to nothing more than a smile on my face and my hand on his head.

This Labrador retriever did not compete in field trials or hunt tests. No initials adorned his name; he was not in demand as a stud. I neither sought nor expected recognition—for him or myself—from the efforts of his life. What he provided in their stead was beyond mere strands of ribbons, the fast-fading shine of trophies, or a few transient dollars.

He offered me what these dogs have in abundance; what Labradors have been offering owners since the breed's arrival on American shores—the ability to deliver moments and days and years of untarnishable memories that rest ever-gleaming on the shelves of the mind.

And those moments that become days and years is what *A Dog For All Seasons* is about. This anthology offers a selection of the experiences, thoughts, and remembrances of sportsmen/writers whose lives, in one fashion or another, have intersected with this splendid breed. The following chapters include histories and small events, humor and lamentations, gains and losses, high times and hard times, hunting and field trial tales. But whatever the thrust of a chapter, each author—in his own style and from his own unique perspective—celebrates the many sides of the Labrador retriever.

CHAPTER ONE

The Labrador Retriever—Who is he?
By Richard A. Wolters

The Labrador is the king of retrievers. He may not be the handsomest or the strongest, but he is the king. He is intelligent but not cunning; he's lovable but not soft. The Labrador retriever is loyal but not a one-man dog. He's gentle but not a dog to be backed against the wall. He's a romping fun fellow but won his crown as an honest worker.

The Lab is as much at home on your bed as he is calmly sitting next to an Illinois pit blind undaunted by a cutting wind. He's the waterfowler's first choice, but he is also a fine upland hunter. He'll give you the sportiest woodcock hunting possible in Maine, and he'll unravel the tricks of Iowa's pheasants. He may not be the fastest swimmer, but if you send him for a crippled goose on the Eastern shore, he won't quit. He's truly the hunter's dog, yet when he comes into this world he doesn't have a hateful gene in his body.

Versatility is the hallmark of the Lab. Police work? No problem. The London Bobbies use Labs all the time. Leading the blind? He outperforms the breed that started the business.

Helping conservationists? He works side by side with game wardens in every state and with scientists in Canada. But the Lab's real conservation efforts are with Harry, Bill, and Joe, the duck hunters, who need his help to protect the bag by making every downed duck count. Ask any waterfowler about Labs, and you will hear stories of courage, persistence, loyalty, and just plain smarts. He can also tell you how the Lab compares with other retrievers: "When a game warden comes around to your blind, the Chesapeake will try to tear his arm off, a Golden will lick his face, but a Lab will show him where you hid the extra ducks or where the bag of corn is kept."

Mallard, canvasback, wood duck, blue-winged teal, or even merganser—the kind of duck makes no difference, nor does it make any difference what flyway he's on. The Lab is as good a worker in Oregon as he is in Louisiana. He can learn the ways of the oak swamp hunters in the Ozarks, run the shoreline and toll the ducks in Nova Scotia, sit quietly in a punt off Chincoteague, scan the skies from the rocks on Long Island Sound, work from a stilt blind on California lakes, or walk at heel in Central Park. And that is really the point with this dog: He can be taught anything that is possible for a dog to learn. He takes to training as easily as any breed and he laps it up. Both in America and in England, he has proven to be such a good worker, so biddable and with such a dependably docile temperament, generation after generation, that it is no wonder the Lab has become the most popular dog in the United States.

Contrary to popular belief, the Labrador retriever did not see the shores of Labrador until modern times; in fact, his name is a fluke, a misnomer derived from the nineteenth-century British concept of geography that lumped Labrador and Newfoundland together in the same land mass. In the same century, the Lab almost became extinct in England because of complex business and political situations, and the same thing almost happened in America during the Great Depression.

In the early 1930s, when the Lab outperformed the Chesapeake Bay retriever in field trials, the American waterfowler took him into the marshes and he has been there ever since. In the field the true test is the field trial, and the record book shows overwhelmingly that if you want to win consistently, you might as well start with Labradors. Other breeds sneak in and win once in a while, but not very often. Hunters call the Lab an "honest" dog; he lives to work. He'll break the Minnesota ice to retrieve a downed bird and shake the crystals off his back after he delivers the bird to hand. Then he's raring to go again when the next flight drops into the decoys. He'll work in the heat of the Texas desert all day gathering doves, and his pay is the retrieve and a pat.

During most of the nineteenth century, the Lab was owned only by a few aristocratic British sportsmen. Although he was introduced to England in the beginning of that century, he was not available to the average British sportsman until the twentieth century. When he was first brought to the United States in the late 1920s, he had much the same history—used by only a very few wealthy sportsmen and then only in the traditional British hunting manner.

Credit must be given to two sources for keeping the Labrador breed alive: (1) the aristocratic families and their gamekeepers in both England and America, and (2) the American sportsmen who gradually "adopted," developed, and trained the dog for their hunting needs. Though American waterfowlers had a good hunting dog, the Chesapeake retriever, the Lab proved to be a better dog for them—and their families.

The Labrador has proven to be a strong breed, passing down his attractive qualities through hundreds of years. From his days in Newfoundland he has passed on his traits as a "workaholic," and from his earliest days in England, his wonderful temperament.

The temperament of the Labrador retriever is an enigma. A dog tends to assume his temperament from the nature of his environment or the characteristics of his people. For example, the Eskimo dog is a tough dog in his native habitat and illustrates the principle of the survival of the fittest: He will kill for food. His temperament comes from his environment; he is not a house pet. The Doberman Pinscher, on the other hand, adopted the character of his masters—Prussian military officers who commanded strong, one-man loyalty. Neither dog could be considered for babysitting duties.

The Labrador's ancestors were developed in Newfoundland, which has the harshest environment settled by any Europeans in North America. The conditions under which they lived made the lives of the Pilgrims seem rich by comparison. The dog's heritage began in sub-survival living conditions, which should produce a rough temperament. The dog's first job in Newfoundland was working with the fishermen from Devon, England, who were considered the roughest, toughest men of Britain. The first settlers on the island were ship-jumpers and deserters from the British fishing fleet and the navy, a lawless society that defied any authority. Yet from this raw society the even-tempered St. John's dog, the direct ancestor of the Labrador, was developed.

To solve the mystery of the Labrador's ancestry, we must thoroughly investigate not only the history of the dog but also the history of his owners and the times in which they lived. This is no easy task, for there were no men of letters to record the dog's earliest days in Newfoundland. In fact, the dog was not mentioned in English sporting literature until the early nineteenth century.

Puzzling history or no, we are lucky. We have the dog today, almost five hundred years from his modern beginnings. Documenting his past, loving his presence, and looking toward his future is an exciting, challenging, intellectual gambit—and a celebration of the Labrador retriever.

CHAPTER TWO

Backwater's Morning Harpsichord
By Bob Butz

Right now, I can no more deny the urge to hunt than a salmon can stop itself from swimming upstream in the fall. Yet I wonder sometimes if this hunger, this thing that pulls in the gut, will loosen its grip on me over time. I wonder if I will ever mind the cold, the rain and wind in my face, or be too weak in the knees to wade in the muck. Will I become a hunter of memory, one of those old men who sit around and lament with that tired talk about the way things used to be?

I'm only twenty-eight, too young, you might say, to have given old age much thought. But the men die young in my family, so the truth is, I've thought a lot about growing old.

I suppose I was in one of these melancholy moods (my wife, Nancy, calls them *funks*) when it came time to choose a name for our puppy; Backwater's Morning Harpsichord was to be an allusion—a poetic reference to the marsh's music at dawn.

When I was twelve or thereabouts, a sunrise on the opening day of duck season was something not to be enjoyed but rather endured until it was light enough for the shooting to start. But over the years and with every new opening day, sunrise on the marsh sounds more and more like a symphony to my ears: it's in the whistle of duck wings; the distant, mournful honking of a goose; a slight breeze blowing across the water like a moonlit whisper. The dog's name was born from remembrances of that and, admittedly, from my own personal touch of artistic flair.

We called him Harper for short, making sure in the beginning that this new moniker was not used in conjunction with any reprimand. Instead, it became a heralding for everything good in his world, be it a cheery calling to the food bowl or a beckoning to come and play.

We carted him all the way from Wisconsin without a care or clue as to what we'd call him—the name came later. We hurried him home from Monticello during a gale, across the Upper Peninsula of Michigan, and over the Straits of Mackinac. Nancy slept most of the way, the puppy stretched lengthwise on her lap, out cold. In the quiet, I found myself going back over the months preceding, in a sense, already plotting against this little pup.

It was strategy I considered, for above all else I wanted a hunting dog that would be better than any I'd brought up so far. And to ensure that, and in an effort not to repeat some of the many mistakes I'd made in the past, I'd watched countless videos and read what now seemed like too many books on dog training.

What I mean is that two dog trainers rarely agree on anything. But no matter; there would be no formal training on the docket for the first couple weeks. We would all bond, as they say. At most he would learn the meaning of *No*; learn that shoes, carpet corners, and the legs of kitchen chairs were not for chewing. We wanted him to get comfortable with us, to feel safe. So we took him for long drives, took him for walks on the busy sidewalks downtown. He especially enjoyed the forays to the park, where he was allowed to chase the flightless, mutant park ducks that loitered there.

In the snow, I shoveled out a toilet space in the backyard and borrowed a phrase from one of my training books. *Hurry up! Hurry up!* became the mantra for Harper doing his thing. Mostly, though, he let go in the house whenever and wherever it pleased him—especially in his crate, a place he despised totally and defiled numerous times a day.

But a puppy should be crate-trained, especially a hunting dog. Though it may bother many dog lovers, it was for us the only way to keep him out of trouble during the day. My wife and I work for a living, but for the record, we no doubt would have acclimated him to the crate anyway. As it was, we came home for long lunches. We even took vacation time to spend as many of those early days with the puppy as we could. After a couple of weeks, the whining and barking behind the latched crate door slowly abated. He never would fancy the place, though; he merely tolerated it.

Harper exhibited a propensity for picking up things from the moment we brought him home. In those first days, I wanted more than anything to ball up a sock and pitch it across the room just to see the outcome. But I staved off the notion. No sense rushing into things, I thought.

9

• • •

It's hard to say what would have driven my father crazier—my growing library of dog training books or those ten-minute training sessions twice a day. I can see him now, rolling his eyes and pleading to the heavens, "For Pete's sake, boy. It's a damn dog." My father—a man who never, in my recollection, formally trained a hunting dog in his life—probably rolled over in his grave a hundred times during the course of Harper's early education.

But Harper proved a most willing and eager student, no matter how clumsy or ham-handed the lesson. In him, I was soon to discover an uncanny mix of intelligence, tenacity, and desire—the kind of dog whose potential was bound only by what I was ready to demand of him.

Nash Buckingham once wrote, "The best long range duck load is a trained retriever." Unlike the pointing breeds, which hold the birds until the hunter can casually stroll up, flush, and pot them, a Labrador's duty is not only to find the birds, but also to flush them into the air for the gun. Then, he is to find and bring to hand any fallen birds, those either wounded or killed by the hunter.

This drive to retrieve, and in fact hunt, is something born into them; it cannot be taught. But in a puppy, the desire lacks focus, is unrefined, and is often misdirected. In the beginning, it's a frantic, uncontrollable oral fixation they have not only to carry but also to gnaw and shred everything except the carload of chew toys you bought specifically for this purpose.

To safeguard the pup's enthusiasm for retrieving, the experts advise never to bellow at him, or otherwise berate him at the top of your lungs should the little bugger amble up to you with the tattered remains of a dress shoe in his mouth. Instead, you are advised to tell him what a good boy he is while gently prying the remains from his razor-sharp, gnashing teeth. Exchange it, then, for something more appropriate for chewing, and tell him again what a good boy he is. Admonish him only if he should amble back to the closet to recoup your loafers.

Like most Labrador puppies, Harper was a terror from the outset. Discovering him to be fearless and fiercely obstinate in the weeks leading up to his formal training, I thought that I was hopelessly over-dogged.

But I saw a subtle change in Harper the day I cordoned off the living room and constructed an alleyway of chairs and a turned-over coffee table. It was the place we would start our retrieving work. I rescued an old sock he had pilfered from the laundry basket, stuffed it with its mate, knotted the end, and positioned myself at the open end of the chute. This way, say the experts, the pup has nowhere to run but toward you, hopefully with the makeshift dummy in his mouth.

But before I sat poised to chuck it down the line, I held him close against my side. He squirmed only for a moment, until I shook the "bumper" in front of him. Suddenly, he was transfixed. Mesmerized. The toss was short, an easy mark. But the outcome was cause for a grand celebration.

He went after it and picked it up like a linebacker going after a fumble. I was already calling him in, patting the floor with both hands and blabbering a quick, staccato succession of *Heres*. With nowhere to run, he stopped, eyeing the low walls of the chute and me, the maniac rolling around on the floor blocking his only escape.

When he came, he came fast—head down like a tiny black bull. I have no way of knowing, but I suppose I will be as happy when my children take their first steps. With a leap of faith, he launched himself the last couple of feet. And my arms opened wide to receive him.

CHAPTER THREE

A Dog's Best Friend
By Robert F. Jones

The clamor is faint at first, querulous and questioning as they lift off the river half a mile away, then louder as the flock nears the set. Jake raises his heavy, anvil-shaped head from my knee and searches the sky. He knows this sound means impending action, but can he in some mysterious way also understand the aerial dialogue? He's a Labrador, so I wouldn't be a bit surprised.

Louder, closer, losing altitude now as they circle, all their yammer drowns out thought—but it's becoming "happy talk" as the geese let their appetites take charge. Unmistakable, that sound: a confident, anticipatory chatter as the Canadas assure one another that everything will be dandy once they've touched down.

But in the dark, dank pit blind, tension mounts. The dog is shivering uncontrollably now, his eyes rolled skyward toward the light that filters in through small gaps in the camouflage. This is a critical moment. If Jake yips only once, the geese might flare off. Shadows flicker over us, big ones, accompanied by the winnowing sound of strong wings hissing overhead. Jake is pressing himself tight and hot against my leg. Joe Judge, my host and shooting partner, wisely refrains from any further calling. It's the last weekend of the season, and at such close range the slightest sour note could turn the flock away from us. Joe's eyes, too, are straining upward, waiting for that final moment when the flock sets its wings in commitment to the spread. My hand is tight on the lever that controls the sliding roof of the pit blind. Like Jake, I'm shivering—but not from the cold.

"Now!"

I yank the lever and the roof whooshes open. Suddenly we're on our feet, guns swinging automatically to our shoulders, unwilled, without thought.

The sky is solid with swirling Canadas caught with their flaps down.

I swing on a big gander—his black paddles spread downward for the landing, beady eyes bright black, his pale gray breast roseate in the sunrise light—then check my swing at the last moment. *Too tough to chew* is my first conscious thought in twenty minutes. Instead, I switch to a younger bird struggling to regain flight speed, primaries spread like fingers to claw at the frosty air. At my shot, the bird folds and thuds on the frozen earth, bounces once in the dry corn stubble, and lies still. Joe's Browning bellows at the far end of the blind. I see the glint of brass and red plastic as he shucks an empty, then I'm swinging smoothly on a goose that's almost back to speed, moving away from me at a slight left-to-right angle. From the edge of my vision I see Joe swing on another bird, off to the far left. We fire simultaneously—

both birds topple and bounce. We look at each other and smile, eyes locked and happy.

Jake is standing on the bench, solemn and hot-eyed, watching me for the signal. I swing my hand outward.

"Fetch 'em, boy!"

He's out of the pit like a blond muzzle blast—a big, strong, pantherine dog doing what he was born to do. He pays no heed to the stuffers and silhouettes arrayed around the pit. His eyes seek only the downed birds, the real thing. He runs past the first one—a single glance tells him it's stone dead, not going anywhere. He can fetch it later. Farther out, about forty yards from the blind, a goose is still struggling in the cornstalks. Jake scoops it up at a run, hardly slowing, turns on a dime, and shifts the big bird in his wide-stretched mouth so that it balances evenly from his grip across its back. Head high, tail wagging, he gallops back to where I'm standing, still in the blind. He drops the goose right in front of me and turns to run left, toward Joe's birds.

In that moment I swear that he winks at me, then grins as he moves off to finish the job.

• • •

It would be gratifying to say I taught Jake all that he knows—his steady, silent discipline in the blind, his eagerness to retrieve, his knowledge of which birds to deal with first once they're on the ground, and the uncanny ability to mark all the downed birds the instant he's out of the blind. But the more I hunt, whether for uplands or waterfowl, the more I'm convinced that the most important element in the making of a good gun dog is not hard-core force training inspired by fear, but rather a constant, almost symbiotic companionship fueled by the dog's innate desire to please.

This will be Jake's fourth season, and already he's the best gun dog I've ever owned. Through the years—more than forty seasons—I've hunted over setters, Brittanies, German shorthairs, Chessies, and a whole laboratory of Labs, but never one so quick to learn. It sometimes seems to me that Jake didn't have to learn at all: He knew it all from the moment he saw a shotgun.

The irony is that Kent Hollow Jake, to give him his proper American Kennel Club name, comes almost entirely from bench stock. I live in Vermont, but got him from a breeder in Zeeland, Michigan, at the suggestion of a friend who'd recently lost his nonhunting yellow Labrador bitch and thought it would be nice if we both had pups from the same litter.

I admit that I was leery of yellow Labs bred primarily for show. Most of my previous experience had been with black Labradors from field bloodlines. I'd had a yellow Lab years earlier, a big, hardheaded dog named Simba who'd been only fair-to-middling in the field, eager enough and a radar-nosed retriever, but hardmouthed much of the time. I mainly hunted the northeastern uplands in those days. Grouse, woodcock, and pheasant were our stock in trade, and Simba always insisted on crunching the first bird of the season—often the last as well, and maybe a few in the middle. But then, I'd picked him up almost haphazardly when he was already a year and a half old, from a British couple who were moving back to Blighty and didn't want to subject the dog to the long imprisonment of quarantine required by British immigration law.

Twenty years later, I once again had a good gun dog, a black Lab named Luke with a multichampion field background. I'd trained him from puppyhood on both upland birds and ducks, and he could literally read my mind. But Luke had worked hard all his life and when he was eleven years old, I knew he only had a couple more seasons in him at best. Perhaps if I got a pup while Luke was still hunting, the old dog could teach the pup a few subtle things that were beyond my all-too-paltry human skills. Maybe he could even teach a *yellow* bench Lab how to hunt!

We started Jake on upland birds the first day he arrived at his new home. He was still wobbly on his outsized paws, but Luke's keen spirit struck a spark in the pup that quickly blazed to a five-alarm fire. Before he was three months old, Jake was flushing woodcock regularly and even a partridge or two. Luke kept a lock on all the retrieving chores, though. Only in Jake's second season would the older dog allow him to fetch.

Jake had been whelped in August, so I didn't start him on waterfowl until that second season when he was just over a year old. By then he'd already become a fine flushing dog, but I worried that as a result of all the fast-moving upland work, he'd be restless in a blind—one of Luke's few faults. The old dog was such a charger that he often whined and fidgeted in a blind, sometimes even yipping uncontrollably just as ducks or geese were about to pitch in. He always looked properly guilty after he'd done so, but he just couldn't help himself, nor could I break him of the fault.

Fearful that Luke would transmit this bad habit to Jake (even as he'd transmitted so many good ones), I regretfully left the old dog at home that year when I went down to Joe Judge's place for the early duck season—Jake's first.

Joe's Twin Ponds Duck Club is one of the finest waterfowl venues I've ever had the pleasure to shoot. Countless ducks—some of them returnees from the twenty-five thousand mallards Judge has banded and released over the years—and up to a quarter of a million Canada geese use the immediate area during the fall and winter. In an era marked by increasingly woeful waterfowl shooting on the Atlantic Flyway, Judge has managed, through canny habitat improvement and judicious oversight, to retain much of the richness of the area's legendary past.

Well before sunup the next day, Joe parked his truck at the edge of the Chester River and we hiked through the dark with Jake at heel. Wind from the north at thirty knots—Spartina thrashed and surf boomed on the rocks, sloshing and foaming at our feet—cold as the gunmetal dawn just breaking. Jake had never seen a johnboat before but he jumped in at my command. The blind too, when we got there, seemed as familiar to him as our living room back home. It was as if he'd been there many times before, and perhaps he had been, somewhere in the depths of the wondrous Labrador gene pool.

Luckily, action came quickly that morning. Too long a wait might have made Jake fidget. Across the bay I saw a raft of ducks lift skyward into the first light for their breakfast feed. "Get ready," Joe said. "Here they come." He began to call.

18

Jake perked his ears at the strengthening gabble of duck talk, the whistle of wings getting louder as the flight approached. Luke might have been whining and yipping by now, unable to control himself. But the young dog lay steady; only shivers betrayed the excitement he felt. Even his eyebrows were shivering. But he kept his head down, eyes averted almost purposely from the first ducks—greenheads and baldpates—that slashed overhead and circled back into the dekes. I looked up and saw them, cupped for the touchdown. We rose and opened fire.

When the smoke cleared and I opened the door of the blind, Jake was out like a shot. He'd seen the angles we'd been shooting at and stared out over the water to mark the fallen ducks. At Joe's hand signal, he hit the water with a long, leaping splash and swam strongly through weed and breaking waves—pausing only once to grab at a decoy, which he quickly rejected (he never bothered a decoy again). All told, Jake brought in twenty-five ducks that weekend, both for us and for others hunting Joe's water. He handled cripples as deftly and gently as he did dead birds.

Later in the season, when we came down for geese, I witnessed his first confrontation with a big, broken-winged honker. The gander stood taller than Jake, hissing as formidably as a king cobra, one wing extended in a clublike threat display. Jake studied the bird for a moment, feinted to his left, then ducked around to the right behind the goose and grabbed it by the root of its good wing. That was a tactical error, as he soon learned, because as he brought it into the field blind, its dragging weight pulled him around in a series of awkward loops. We went out and showed him how to grasp the bird across the back, pinning its wings to its sides, a lesson he's never forgot.

"You've got a good dog," Joe said—high praise indeed.

• • •

Jake was bred for looks, not hunting ability. How then can I account for his considerable talents in the field and, more significantly, the speed with which he learned to use them? Was his keenness to hunt already there when I got him, immersed in his bloodlines, or was he motivated to hunt by contact (and perhaps competition) with Luke? As to tactics, Luke certainly taught him a lot—but only about upland game. How did he get so smart so fast when we got around to waterfowl?

I firmly believe it's a Labrador's innate desire to please that makes him such a quick study. No other breed, in my experience, is quite so playful, quite so eager to learn the games its master plays, or quite so happy when he gets it all right. If that's true, then my instinctively laid-back, low-key training methods, developed over years of gun dog ownership, have added up to the correct regimen.

I've spent long hours with Jake right from the start at such "games" as obedience, retrieving, and actual bird hunting. I talk to him a lot so that he recognizes my tones of voice—praiseful, warning, remonstrative, excited, or good-humored. I maintain eye contact with him as much as I can—he now feels the weight of my gaze even when his back is to me. In turn, he watches me and, from my unconscious body language and facial expressions, he has learned to anticipate most of my wishes. When he does what

I want, I reinforce what I've taught him with lavish praise and plentiful petting. I try to anticipate his thought processes and his next move, distracting him if it's something I don't want him to do, encouraging him if it is.

If I'm seated somewhere and he's beside me, which inevitably he is, I'll reach down from time to time even when I'm doing something else and pat his head, grab him by the muzzle, and let him chew on my fingers, warning him with a growled *No!* if his jaws close too tightly. Thus, he's learned to be soft-mouthed when he picks up something that belongs to me, whether it's my hand or a duck I've shot.

As a result of this mutual attention we pay one another, I can literally read his mind and he's learned to read mine. In short, I've become my dog's best friend and I never let him forget it.

CHAPTER FOUR

Upland Passage
By Robert F. Jones

If life were fair, hunters and their gun dogs would have identical life spans—learning, peaking, and declining together, step for step, one man, one dog hunting along the same trail of time toward the same destination. But it doesn't work that way. Few hardworking hunting dogs last more than a dozen seasons. Then time catches up with them, rewarding their diligence with arthritis, cataracts, cysts, tumors, and just plain old age.

But the good ones never lose their passion for the field. Nothing is sadder for the hunter than seeing his old dog, lame and white-muzzled with his tail still going like a runaway metronome, as the man takes down his gun for an outing he knows the dog cannot endure. The dog stares up with clouded eyes, pleading.

"No, boy," the man says. "Not anymore. You stay home and rest."

Over the course of a career spanning eleven bird seasons, my grizzled black Labrador, Luke, had just gotten better and better. In Vermont, where I live, those seasons run roughly ninety days long, from the last Saturday in September through the end of the year, and they had been the high points of our lives. Luke lived for the fall, and I for the joy it gave him.

Seeing a dog learn and refine his skills as a hunter is more rewarding to me than killing a limit of grouse and woodcock every day of the season. Once Luke had learned all I could teach him about flushing and retrieving game birds, he began teaching me. I learned to trust his infallible nose, which could find birds where I wouldn't have believed they could be. I learned to follow him, on faith alone, into the really hard country—steep, over-grown hillsides bristling with thorns; muck-bottomed marshes that can suck your boots off; blizzard-whipped apple orchards where naked branches poke at your eyes and grouse get up with a roar of wings as loud as the storm but disappear, usually, before you can raise the gun. From Luke I learned persistence, endurance, stoicism, loyalty, and not a little bit about love.

By our fifth season together, I began to notice that more birds than ever were flushing directly back to me. At first I thought it was coincidence, but I began to make note of the flush-backs in my gunning diary. Over the next six seasons, Luke flushed a total of 1,078 birds (567 woodcock, 511 ruffed grouse); 63 percent of them flew toward or past my gun.

I had always been able to tell when Luke was getting "birdy": his strong otterine tail would come up and start flailing faster; he would glance over at me, wherever I was moving through the cover, to make sure I had my eye on him; his thick coat, shiny already, seemed to light up from within and throw blue-black glints as his guard hairs rose. During his fifth season, however, he added a new tactic to his hunting repertoire. I noticed him purposely circling out beyond where he'd located the bird, then pussyfooting in on it, his nostrils flared as he inhaled its rich scent, to end with a pouncing rush that flushed the bird. More often than not, it flew my way.

I'd like to say my marksmanship is as good as Luke's flushback rate, but it's not. Over the years, I've rarely hit more than 40 percent of the game birds I've shot at. When I missed, Luke would look back at me with disappointed eyes. All that work for nothing.

"Gone away, boy," I might say rather lamely.

He would merely shrug and forge on.

When I connected, though, he was in his element—retrieving. Sharp-eyed as always, he marked where the bird had fallen and leaped after it: into muddy swamp edges, barbed thickets of multiflora rose, dense brakes of doghair aspen or maple whips, through ice-fringed rushing brooks, even a few times in the late season into snowdrifts as deep as his shoulders. Luke always got his bird. If it was down, it was ours. There was always pride in his bearing when he brought back a bird I'd shot, and gentleness in the jaws that held it.

Once we were working through a patch of old apple trees, for grouse. At the far end, Luke got birdy in some whippy brush and pushed out a woodcock. I fired just as the bird turned a corner around a big maple tree that was still in full leaf. It seemed to me that I had missed. The afternoon was hot. Luke and I were both breathing hard, so I told him, "Let's take a break." He seemed reluctant, but he sat, edgy, muttering, eager. Ten minutes later, we pushed on, around the maple tree where I'd fired at the woodcock. Luke stopped about five yards behind me, peered at the ground, then looked up at me doubtfully. "Come on," I said, a bit sharply. "Hunt 'em up, hunt 'em up!" Again he seemed to shake his head, again looked at the ground before him. I went back to where he stood. There lay the woodcock I had shot at ten minutes earlier. "Okay," I said, embarrassed. "Fetch." He fetched and gave, the ritual complete. I never loved him more. We hunted on.

But time—"that old bald cheater," as Ben Jonson called it—deals down and dirty with all of us. By the summer of 1989, I realized that Luke would have to hang up his bell collar pretty soon. His left shoulder was arthritic, the bounce was fading from his rear suspension, and his eyes were growing hazy blue with incipient cataracts. After all, he was eleven years old. I could handle the arthritis by feeding him an aspirin wrapped in raw hamburger before we went out each day; the spring would return to his stride as the season wore on and he put more up-and-down miles behind him; his nose would make up in keenness for what his eyes had lost. More disconcerting was a new problem: Over the winter and spring, he had developed a hacking, half-strangulated cough that wouldn't go away. His bark sounded broken, like a teenage boy's voice when it's changing; his breath came raspy at the best of times.

"Laryngeal paralysis," my sure-handed local vet said once she had studied Luke's chest and throat X-rays. "His bark box—his larynx—is paralyzed. Nobody knows what causes it, but it happens, most commonly in racehorses. They call them 'roarers.' I'll give him something for it, a cortisone-based drug called prednisone. Just a five-milligram pill every other day. It can't cure the problem, but at least it'll relieve the inflammation, make it easier for him to swallow."

"Can I hunt him?"

"Sure," she said, tousling Luke's ears as he looked gravely up at her. She often rode her horses near coverts we hunted, along a wild, wooded ridge just back of town. Sometimes she would tell me where she had seen grouse dusting or feeding. She knew what Luke was made of—all heart.

"Bird hunting," she told him now. "That's what you live for, isn't it?"

His ears perked, and his tail thumped: *Yes, indeed!*

• • •

Why, you might ask (and many have), would a dedicated upland bird hunter prefer a Lab to the more surefire pointing breeds? Wouldn't a more traditional dog such as an English setter or pointer, a German shorthair or a Brittany—actually the dog of choice in my part of New England—produce more birds for you? Of course it would; but not the way I like to hunt them. I certainly admire the control and walking-on-eggs caution a good pointing dog exercises in his craft, but I'm not out for a high body count. I much prefer the spontaneity of hunting behind a flushing dog. There's a kind of existential rhythm to pounding along fast behind your dog, seeing him get birdy, tail going like mad, then having him check back to make sure you are ready before he plunges in to flush the bird. It all happens so suddenly. The birds seem to materialize out of nothingness, already moving fast, and are as quickly gone, or dead. You learn to shoot from any position. You may not get as many shots or hit as many birds as you do with a pointer, but you never lose cripples that might elude a less effective retriever than a Labrador.

And anyway, I just love Labs. The ones I've known over the years have had a greater sense of fun and retained it longer after puppyhood than any other breed I'm familiar with. I can see many moods in a Labrador's eyes—seriousness, resentment, anticipation, anxiety, sometimes gravity, sometimes even scorn or contempt, but most often love and its jolly twin, playfulness. Am I being anthropomorphic—attributing human emotions to a creature incapable of them? Perhaps; but then, I'm an anthropoid.

I'm not the only Lab fancier to find a nearly human quality in these dogs. In his *Recollections of Labrador Life*, first published in 1861, a traveler named Lambert de Boilieu had this to say of the breed: "The Labrador dog, let me remark, is a bold fellow, and, when well taught, understand, almost as well as any Christian biped, what you say to him."

I once calculated that my second Lab, Simba, had a vocabulary in excess of one hundred words. My wife and I had to resort to Spanish or German when debating if and when we were going to take him for a walk/hike/stroll/jaunt/perambulation/constitutional/promenade/saunter/ramble/traipse, or stretch of the legs. Even at that, it took him only a week to equate *paseo* and *Spaziergang* with all of the above.

"I think I'll remove the *perro amarillo* from the premises for a brief *paseo* before retiring." Arf, arf, whine, whine—and a whirlwind dash toward the back door.

Luke, on the other hand, could read my mind, I swear. I'd be sitting upstairs at the typewriter in my office, with a few hundred words painfully pecked out, when my thoughts would stray to the bird covers: Which ones should we hunt today? Better give the ridge a rest—we hit it pretty hard yesterday. Maybe Dorset Mountain? No, it's Saturday—could be flatlanders in there. How about the Woodcock Islands up the road; we haven't been there in a while, and flight birds may have arrived . . .

Heavy breathing from the foot of the stairs, followed by a tentative moan. Then the slow clump of footsteps up the stairway. Luke's head peeks around the corner of the banister. His eyes lock on mine, then shift to the gun cabinet across from my desk. His eyes hold the question. Mine answer, involuntarily. . . . And he's dancing on the carpet, lit up like a hunk of anthracite, his eyes sparking with joy. Drumming up enthusiasm.

I could say *No!* and he'd slink away downstairs to mumble and mutter doggy curses at the unfairness of it all. The birds *are* there; he knows it from the weather, from the cocky tang in the air, the hum of the planets, the stare of the moon last night. How can I deny him? I take down the shotgun and reach for my boots . . .

Luke's job and mine are one: Together we kill game birds. Nothing else matters; not sex or food or comfort, not sleep or warmth, water or love. We're not merely a "team," man and dog, but a single being with a single-minded mission: to pound the hills forever, through briers and cold and muck and barbed wire, putting birds up in a roar of wings and knocking them down again with a bang and reek of gunpowder, fetching back the warm bird and stuffing it into a cold game pocket, stained black with bird blood these many years. Later we eat them.

At moments like this, Luke is all business, and so am I. We're driven by the same gods or demons; the wolf is revealed in all his cruel glory. Without Luke I'd be a dilettante. With him I'm a hunter. We transcend ourselves—he's more than a dog, I'm more than a man. Hunting alone, I would leave most of these birds unharmed, unseen perhaps, certainly unflighted. Left to his own devices, he would fly them, all right, but they'd never fall. Together we both fly them and fell them, interrupt the arc, break the rainbow, prove the Second Law of Thermodynamics and yet disprove it at the same time. These birds we kill fly on in my dreams, and in Luke's dreams, too. In sleep, our legs twitch in synchrony, old muscles now, bone-stiff and bone-weary. Blood crusts on his thorn-ripped nose; blood scabs on my thorn-ripped hands.

Yes, I love Labs.

CHAPTER FIVE

Changing Needs
By Joe Arnette

The blind was wrapped in dark, thick quiet broken only by the awakenings of distant geese. Close in, there were more immediate sounds—the rustlings of clothes and shufflings of ponderous boots, the dull thunk of a dropped shotgun shell, breathy snuffs from a young Labrador testing the morning breeze.

Within the pit, the two men were nothing to each other but bulky shapes, sensed more than seen across the few feet that separated them. They were strangers thrown together by chance for a few hours. They had said good morning at breakfast, eaten quietly, and spoken little during the ride to the field. One was right-handed, while the other was a lefty, so spotting themselves in the blind needed few words.

By nature, neither man was outgoing or talkative, especially with strangers. If it hadn't been for the Labrador sitting outside, at the blind's edge, each man would have been content to shoot geese and keep talk to a minimum. It surprised them both when they struck up a conversation.

31

A wooden kitchen match burned away the darkness for an instant, then paused in front of a middle-aged, weather-creased face. "Do you mind if I smoke?" a gravelly voice asked around a pipe stem. "I won't if it bothers you."

"Doesn't bother me at all." The voice was rapid-fire, younger sounding, and disembodied in the murky pit. "I quit a couple of months ago and still crave the smell." A second match flared and died to a glow, then the rich fragrance of tobacco drifted over the blind. A pair of violent sneezes erupted from the Labrador, followed by watery, nose-clearing snorts. His owner chuckled. "Seems Jack doesn't appreciate good Burley. Don't worry about it."

"Sometimes I forget how rough tobacco must be on a dog's nose," the smoker said, shelving his pipe next to an open box of shells. "I'll wait 'til the wind kicks up a touch." His head gesture toward the Lab went unseen in a predawn that was just hinting at daylight, but his words were sharply defined.

"I've always liked the name Jack for a dog. It's simple, to the point, and not foolish. I've used it twice over the years, and one of those Jacks was the best Labrador I've ever owned." He hesitated, as if he was tossing something around in his mind, and then added abruptly, "Or ever will own."

The building clamor of geese had Jack up on his toes, his neck stretched, as he tried to sort out the raucous noise flowing in from all directions. The dog's head whipped sharply upward at the wing whistles of a flock of ducks beating over the decoys. He whined lightly, twice, before his owner put a hand on his back and said, *Quiet*, then *Down*. Both commands were barely above a whisper. The Lab dropped instantly onto a pile of camouflage netting alongside the pit. Other than brief scratchings as he settled in, he did not move or make another sound.

"He's a youngster, not quite two," the man said apologetically. "He's hard-headed and has a lot to learn, but Jack is going to be a good one." He flipped up his collar and tucked the tandem of lanyard-hung whistles into his parka. "In fact, I haven't decided if he is too good a field-trial prospect to hunt, or too good a gun dog not to hunt. That's why I brought him this morning."

The wind was shifting, easing around at an angle behind them and blowing away from the dog. There was the sparking snap of a match, and pipe smoke lofted on the freshening breeze. It rose into a sky smudged by contrasting fingers of gray and blotched with dingy wet clouds, a sky now light enough to show a sprawl of land as bleak as a front porch to nowhere. Wavering strings of ducks and stiff lines of geese were stacked high on the faint streak of horizon.

The older man drew softly on his pipe, looked past his hunting partner, and stared hard at the Labrador, still half-hidden in the gloom. His eyes ran knowingly over the dog, from the profile of its squared-up head, down the muscled shoulders and rump, to the slightly wagging tip of thick tail. He said, "Even lying down, Jack's a fine-looking Labrador. As nicely built as I've seen in some years."

At his name, the dog turned his head, thumped his tail, then went back to sky watching. "Sounds like you know Labradors," Jack's owner said.

"I've had Labs for more than twenty-five years," the other hunter answered, nodding his head. "And nothing but them for most of that time." The man scratched his cheek, his fingers rasping against morning stubble. "I raised and trained my own line for a while—a small operation, just a litter every year or so. I trialed some of my top dogs."

His voice paused, then lowered, as though he had surprised himself with his words. "Actually, I was into the whole trial game seriously for about fifteen years."

"Do you mind telling me your name?" the younger man asked.

At the answer he said, "I've heard about you and your Labradors. The word around the circuit is that they were first-class dogs." There was a touch more respect in his tone when he asked, "Did you quit trialing for any particular reasons?" Then he caught himself and added, "That may not be any of my affair."

"Let's just say that I got tired of nearly everything that went with hard training and stiff competition. It wasn't the dogs; I still love the breed, maybe more than ever. But now I have them—just a couple—for what they are, not for what they can do." He hesitated, looked again at the alert Labrador, then seemed to come to a decision.

"I've not talked about this with many people," the man said in a subdued voice. "I suppose the reason I'm telling you is that you're a stranger I'll never see again, and if you run the national trial circuit you've likely heard the story anyway.

"That Jack dog I mentioned," he continued, "the best I've ever owned? I ruined him—killed him in the end, if I'm being truthful—trying to win it all at a big trial. It was heat stroke. I pushed him too hard, too long, on too hot a day. When I carried him off the field, I swore that I'd never do that, or anything like that, to another dog. He spent two weeks in a clinic and came out of it with heart and brain damage. He lived less than a year. During that time, he could barely walk from the kennel to the house. Then he didn't know where he was when he got there."

The man went on, hurriedly, talking more to himself than the stranger across the blind. "After Jack died, I found homes for my Labs and tore down my whole kennel. I kept two of the softest-tempered, least-talented dogs and brought them into the house to live with me. I expect nothing from them other than happy companionship and picking up a bird now and again when we hunt alone. It may seem strange to you, at your point in life, but I've never been as content or enjoyed dogs more than I do these days."

"You're right," the other man broke into the wordless lull that followed. "I have heard the story. And I'm sorry about your dog, but things like that happen. It's no reason to quit what you love." He pointed at his dog, fully focused on the birds starting to fill the sky, and spoke emphatically. "If I lost this dog today, as much as I care about him, I'd be running another one tomorrow."

"I saw it that way too, years ago, but not anymore," the older man said, between puffs on his dark-stained pipe. "Things don't just happen; we make them happen, or worse, let them happen. And, in all honesty, I'm not sure how much I loved the training and trialing. At first, maybe, until competition became an obsession, and I blurred the line between what I was winning and what

I was losing. When my dogs became nothing more than living means to a dead end, there was a kennel full of reasons to quit.

"Don't get me wrong," he followed up quickly, in an effort to smooth over any tension he might have created. "I love to watch well-handled, high-powered dogs—especially up-and-coming youngsters like your Jack. I just don't own or train them anymore."

He turned away and scanned the gray sky, now dropping soft snow, as if the heavy clouds were crumbling into lighter pieces. "Perfect weather," he said, smiling widely at the younger man. He picked up his shotgun and shoved shells into it, then said, "I can't wait to see Jack in action, but he won't get any work unless I stop talking. Look out there. Low, at about nine o'clock. We've got geese coming in."

CHAPTER SIX

Retriever Tribulations
By Bobby George, Jr.

We motored down the Three-Mile Ditch on the Missouri side of the Mississippi River following another boatload of hunters, all of us part of a watery, moonlit parade.

In front, I could see the lights, now and then a boat turning down one of the slots toward the "E" blinds, then another party of hunters threading through the timber to one of the "F" blinds. The night vibrated with voices, murmuring in the dark. The parade thinned the farther down the ditch we traveled. In the darkness, I could hear ducks splashing and jumping into the black unknown.

The slow boat ride through flooded timber in the dark made me wonder about things I would never think about in the daylight. The darkness and the water are sensitizers, and with that sensitivity comes the realization that man is not equipped to deal with the night.

Pearl the Lab, on the other hand, was right at home. She sat in front of me. She was already wet, having jumped into the ditch as we were loading our gear into the boat. She shivered and test-ed the breeze, edging slowly upward out of the *Sit* command she was supposed to be obeying.

"Sit," I said, following it up with a slap on her behind. She looked quickly back at me, not really startled, more a look of annoyance than one of subservience. She started to inch out of the command again and I just shook my head. We would be going through this all day; no sense hitting my frustration peak too early.

"Okay," I said, letting her out of the command. "Okay, go on."

She immediately scuttled over two huge bags of decoys, walked across a pair of gun cases, and tipped over a cup of coffee on the seat in front of me as she moved to the bow.

Jerel, who was running the bow light, trying his damnedest to keep us off stumps and fallen timber, is the nervous type, and he already had one dog on the bow with him—his little chocolate Lab, Coke. He shouted some profanity as Pearl pushed Coke into him. But Jerel, a veteran of the duck wars and a longtime retriev-er addict, simply stood up, giving the two dogs the bow of the boat. He knew it was just too much trouble, too early, to fight their little battles of attrition. I mean that, sure, we could win in a training session—after all, we had the whips and collars—but the dogs always got even in the end. Somehow, they always outlasted us. The coffee cup, of course, belonged to Jerel. In the residual glow of the big spotlight, I could see that his teeth were clenched so tight that the enamel was starting to splinter.

About that time, Randy, sitting at the tiller, told Jerel to hold that damn light up where he could see, that we were late, that one of those dogs was going to fall in if we didn't get them back, and so on. Jerel, who was already wound pretty tight, stripped a gear and gave Randy several alternatives about where he could go and the mode of transportation he could take to get there.

"Here," he said to me. "You hold the light."

Coke bounced over the decoys, spilling a box of shells into the puddled floor of the boat. She jumped between Jerel and me, licking both of us on the face in one magically quick motion. Jerel hates that.

And as I tried to stand in the boat with the light, I could hear him struggling through the darkness to get to Coke. She was standing with her feet in Randy's lap and he was screaming at Jerel to get his dog under control and all Jerel really wanted to do, anyway, was throw her out and pick her up on the way back to the truck after the hunt.

"Feet up," I kept hearing him mutter. "She's going back with her feet up . . . back of the truck . . . just be able to see her feet sticking up . . ."

Right then, I don't believe you could call any of the three of us dog lovers. I'm not sure you could even call us retriever lovers, although we have a bunch of them. By the way, a "bunch" of retrievers is dog talk for having two dogs more than you've got kennel spaces.

In the darkness, watching the light on the murky water, I thought of the beginning. . . . Ahh, the beginning . . .

• • •

For me, it started when I was twelve years old and my dad

and I jumped a couple of mallards off a flooded sinkhole near Wooldridge, Missouri. One of the birds fell in the water and Dad wound up going over his boots to pick it up. And although we talked about getting a dog to do that work, it never really came to pass until years later when Pearl, the twelve-week-old black puppy, came along.

I should have known early on that I was in for trouble, but I just didn't understand what I was dealing with. And, as long as I was ignorant about dog work, everything went pretty well. I did all the shooting and she did all the retrieving. I really didn't care that she was usually standing in the decoys by the time the birds hit the water. Anyway, she was just a pup. At least that's what we always said, Jerel and Randy and I, until the dogs started getting gray hair in their muzzles. But I digress.

It was the opening weekend of Missouri's 1984 northern zone duck-hunting season when it was made clear to the three of us that retrievers must be trained and under control if they are going to be of any real value, other than ornamentation, on a duck hunt. Pearl had picked up a few birds the year before when she was eight months old, but this was to be the year she started doing the real work. I let her out of the truck that first morning and Glenn, our Truman Lake scout, jumped back and scowled.

"Who brought that damn coyote?"

His comment about Pearl's deviation from the American Kennel Club standard for Labrador retrievers set the tone for the hunt. The weather, like so many opening weekends around Truman Reservoir in west central Missouri, was almost balmy.

After the morning mist burned off the lake, we hunted in shirt-sleeves.

There weren't many mallards in at the time, so the preseason scouting was done for teal and wood ducks. And Glenn had found them. Oh boy, had he found them. A few miles south of Clinton, just off Highway 13, he had located a stand of flooded timber that was serving as kitchen, bedroom, and lounge for several hundred woodies. In the evenings, they came from miles around to bed down in this little stand of trees.

And we waited for them that first evening. We made up a firing line, standing in waders, hidden in the shade of great, gray-black oak trees, long drowned. The water was about waist-deep, so I had Pearl sitting on a fallen tree beside me.

Just before sundown, they came pouring in from every point of the compass, crying, whistling, and sideslipping through the trees, parachuting in from high places. We shot and shot and still they came. Our limits, everyone's limit, lay on the water in a matter of minutes, and the ducks kept coming. And therein was the problem.

After Pearl retrieved the first bird and I sent her back for another, the splashing caused by landing ducks created serious diversions. The same thing was happening with Lindy, Randy's old meat dog, on the other end of the firing line. It was just a matter of good fortune when one of the dogs happened on a dead bird amidst all the live ones swimming around in the trees.

The final stroke, the exclamation mark to our frustration, was inked in by the darkness. We could not see the dogs, or the dead birds. We couldn't even throw rocks at this point to help the dogs mark downed birds. And I could still hear Pearl swimming and crashing through the brush. Woodies whistled and whirred at her. I estimated that we lost half the ducks we shot that evening.

I was angry and frustrated at the dogs and at myself. I felt ignorant and horribly wasteful and I vowed that night, standing knee-deep in a cocklebur patch next to the best wood-duck hole in Truman Lake, that I would never shoot and lose ducks like that again. I would fix this dog somehow. I had read about retrievers that would take hand signals and voice commands to birds that they had not seen fall. By Jove, that's what we needed!

The next spring, Randy, Jerel, and I started attending field trials and talking to professional retriever trainers. And we read books. If memory serves, it was in that year, when Randy and I were deep into the art of teaching our retrievers to "handle," that Lindy was banished forever from the house.

The first strike against her occurred one weekend when Randy was going to have a few friends over for dinner. He had laid the steaks out on the kitchen cabinet and had seasoned them to a fare-thee-well; humming to himself, he stepped outside to check on the charcoal.

Enter house dog, soon-to-be-handling duck dog, Lindy. Front feet on the counter, head cocked a little to one side, she eyed the meat, checked back over her shoulder, slurped up the steaks, and marched quickly through the open door to the basement.

Enter Randy. "Coals are great," he shouted to his wife in the next room. "Let's cook 'em." Then he saw the bare countertop.

"Susan! Susan! What'd you do with the meat?" He went to the refrigerator. No, she hadn't put them in there. He went back outside, scratching his head.

Eventually, they found the bones and a burping Lindy in the basement. She was exiled from the house for several weeks. But the final nail in the doghouse came some months later.

Susan, an Oreo cookie aficionado, had just returned from the grocery store. After she had put the groceries away, she had set the large package of Oreos on the kitchen table for her later attention. She went to the bedroom for just a moment to change clothes.

Padding up from the basement, the villain, Lindy, went directly to the kitchen table, eyed the cookies, and without so much as a thought about the old jailhouse saw, "Don't do the crime if you can't do the time," snatched the whole package. Randy found the wrapper later that evening.

"Susan," he shouted from the basement. "I found your Oreo." Oreo . . . Singular?

Grinning like a possum in a persimmon tree, he bounced up the stairs. Susan met him at the top. Gingerly, between thumb and index finger, he held what was left of the Oreo package. There was one cookie inside, soggy with dog slobber. Poor Lindy; she couldn't choke down the last piece of evidence.

That was the final straw. Lindy was sentenced to the kennel— for life.

Coke, Jerel's dog, was one of Lindy's daughters. Coke would have been the best duck dog the three of us ever had if we had killed all our birds in cornfields or the Sahara Desert. Coke was pretty sure that if God had intended for retrievers to swim, He would have given them fins. That isn't to say that Coke wouldn't pick up ducks. She would. The only trouble was that it might take her till next Tuesday to find the driest route to the bird.

All of them—Lindy, Pearl, and Coke—were related. And they were all what I would call "self-hunters," which means that they did it on their own. They hunted not for their masters, but for themselves. Their desire to retrieve was a lot stronger than their desire to please.

Nevertheless, we did a lot of dog training that year. We trained in the mornings before work, during lunch hours, after work, weekends, and so on. We caught pigeons, we bought all kinds of training equipment, we played in the gun dog stakes held by local field trial clubs. You name it, we did it. We became dog men. Or, at least, that's what we thought.

All three of the dogs seemed to be steady as rocks by the time the dove season rolled around. Dove hunting supplies the first shooting of the fall in Missouri and always provides a good warm-up for both men and dogs prior to the duck season. By this time, the dogs were handling a little bit and, by golly, things were going to be different this year.

Pearl never stayed with me for one dove during that whole season. I wore out several heeling sticks on her. Randy fared only slightly better.

And Coke? I remember seeing her running full bore across a field of corn stubble after a dove that was sailing toward the far side of the field. She was dragging a ten-foot piece of ski rope and attached to the other end was Jerel's dove stool. I can remember wondering dimly if she'd hurt him.

Pearl had to be the worst, though. By the end of the season she would break for the bird when she heard the safety on my shotgun click off.

During that dove season, Randy took his wife hunting with us one day, and while they were sitting in a tree-lined fencerow, she asked him how he could tell who was shooting.

"You just listen," he said.

"For the shots?"

"No, for the dogs. For instance, if Jerel shoots, you'll hear three shots, then 'No! No, Coke! Heel!' And if it's Bob, you'll hear 'Pearl! No . . . No!', then the shots."

• • •

The treetops were becoming silhouettes against the sky when we finally reached the blind we had drawn. The next perilous moment we had to get past was the placement of decoys. Jerel and I left Randy and the two dogs in the blind. When the first decoy hit the water, Pearl did likewise.

"No! No!" Randy shouted. "Here, Pearl. Come here!" It's so embarrassing, hollering at dogs on a duck marsh. The sound travels forever, and you know that there are hunters with perfectly obedient retrieving machines sitting beside them in their blinds, the dogs of which signed and numbered prints are made. The hunters sitting beside these dogs are grunting scornfully at the hapless slobs across the marsh who can't keep their half-breed mongrels at heel.

Pearl took one sniff at a decoy and headed back to the blind. If Jerel had cut the motor, I'm sure I could have heard his temples throbbing.

I took a deep breath and started wondering again. Why? Why have these dogs taken such a hold on me? I spend about half my waking hours trying to figure them out. What makes them tick? Why are some so good and some not worth feeding? Wherein lies the secret? Is it professional training? Is it in the genes? The brain? The heart? Generally speaking, the qualities I like best in a retriever are the qualities I like best in people.

I turned around and smiled at Jerel. Scowling, Jerel shook his head. "We're late, we're late; we've got to get these decoys out. Come on . . . *come on!*"

By the middle of the morning, we had killed a few ducks, missed a few ducks, and the dogs hadn't yet driven Jerel to commit murder/mayhem/suicide. Randy was nodding into sleep down at his end of the blind when Jerel whispered, "Mallards."

Randy snapped to, his call automatically in his mouth. He talked to them, a small group of ten or twelve. They circled. And circled. Half the group landed in the decoys, and Randy dropped his call.

We came up gunning. We had three greenheads down and Coke and Pearl, as usual, were halfway to two of the birds before they hit the water. I got out of the blind to pick up Pearl because it looked like the last greenhead still had a little life left. I took the dead bird from Pearl and sent her for the last duck.

As soon as she got close, he dove. She circled. He popped up beyond the decoys and I tried to handle her back. Amazingly, she took my cast. She spotted the greenhead, which seemed to be gaining strength, and both headed for the far side of the cove about a hundred yards away. I moved down the bank so I could see better.

"She isn't going to catch him, Bob," Jerel said.

I scratched my chin. The duck was obviously going to make it to the standing timber. Although Pearl didn't appear to be gaining any ground on him, she wasn't losing any either. I would give her to the timber, I thought weakly, knowing full well that there wasn't a damn thing I was going to be able to do about it anyway.

"He's in the timber, Bob," Jerel said. "Better call her in."

"Uhh, yeah." I blew the come-in call on the whistle. She didn't even give me a glance. I blew the pea out of the whistle. No response. Randy and Jerel were silent. They knew better than to say anything. First the greenhead disappeared into the timber, then Pearl.

"I guess we better get that damn boat out," Jerel said.

I walked back into the blind. "Naah, let's give her a few minutes. She might come up with him."

"That duck wasn't hit too hard, Bob," Jerel said, looking over his glasses at me. "He was navigatin' pretty good, and there ain't no way Pearl is going to swim through that timber fast enough to catch him."

We waited. No one spoke. Ten minutes passed. I looked at my watch and thought, that couldn't be possible. Ten minutes can be an hour when you're sitting beneath blue, duckless skies, or it can be a matter of seconds when the birds are flying and shooting time is drawing to a close. At the moment it was passing pretty rapidly and my irritation with the dog had escalated into worry. No one had spoken.

"Bob, we got to go get that dog. What if she got hung in some monofilament or an old trotline or something? We should have gotten the boat out a long time ago."

"You're right, Jerel. Let's go."

We motored across the cove to the timber. There was no way to get our eighteen-foot boat through the blowdowns and root wads. We left Randy in the blind and Jerel and I cruised up the edge, almost back to the ditch, and then we made the return trip to the blind.

"Couldn't find her?" Randy said.

Jerel shook his head. Looking at the floor of the blind, I opened my gun to check the shells. Once again, Pearl and I had screwed up. I should have gotten the boat out right after the duck went into the timber. And what then? She still wouldn't have quit on that duck and come back. We might have been a little closer, but that would have had no effect. No; like always, Pearl was on her own.

"There she is," Randy said. She had been in the water for twenty minutes.

Jerel was standing up, a huge smile on his face. I looked over the edge of the blind. Way down the slot, just breaking through the trees and heading our way, was one black Labrador retriever carrying one mallard drake, both still alive and kicking.

48

"Damn her," I huffed, clearing my throat. "You'd think with all the lickings I've given her that she'd mind better." I couldn't hide the relief in my voice. The wind, as I recall, must have blown chaff into my eyes.

I went through the door at the back of the blind to pick her up. She was breathing like a steam engine when she hit the bank. I took the duck; she shook off and, as usual, didn't wait for me to pet her. Pearl was like that. Hard. Affection was for lapdogs, not for her. Back into the blind she went, and when I finally managed to pull myself together and follow her, she was sitting in the dog box, looking out. Waiting for somebody to put another duck on the water.

Jerel finally spoke. "That was a great retrieve, Bob."

"I couldn't call her back, Jerel."

"That's not the point now, is it? You can train 'em to do a lot of things. Maybe somebody could even train her to be steady. But you can't train 'em to do what she just did."

That evening, heading back up the Three-Mile Ditch, I wondered about passion. Passion for doing something, anything, to the limit. I wondered if I had ever pursued anything—work, a hobby, anything—with *real* passion.

Pearl glanced at me from the bow of the boat. Talk to me, Pearl, I thought; tell me how it feels. Teach me. But she only stared at me with those tough, dark eyes. And I understood.

You're on your own, she was saying.

Just like me.

CHAPTER SEVEN

A Dog Named Bernie
By Geoffrey Norman

A bunch of us were sitting around talking about dogs. Hunters like to do this when they aren't hunting—talk about dogs, that is. They tell dog epics in a way that I imagine isn't very far from the way the ancient Greeks used to sit around and tell stories about their warrior heroes. In fact, if you had a big, hard-going Labrador and named him Hector, you could tell of his deeds in iambic pentameter.

Long ago, in the flooded timber
There lived a creature of stout heart
Firm on sit; steady to wing and shot . . .

Well, you get my drift; and anyway, the conversation I have in mind was not about heroic deeds so much as the comic kind. The mood was Aristophanes more than Sophocles, don't you see. The subject was dogs that, while they wouldn't win any trophies at the field trials, sure knew how to leave 'em laughing. People who have never spent any time around field dogs probably don't believe that a dog can have a sense of humor. Anyone who has hunted much with dogs knows otherwise. Emphatically. Some dogs are just born clowns. They can hunt—some of them are good, as a matter of fact—but they live for laughs.

"You know," one of the men at the table said, "I had an old black Lab, several years back. Male. Name of Mose. That old dog was like one of those comedians who make a living bumping into things or falling down. Mose couldn't get out of his own way. Walked right through the screen door to our kitchen one time, just like it wasn't there. That dog drove my wife right straight up the wall."

"Some women are like that," one of the philosophers said. A medievalist, probably.

"Yeah," the tale teller continued, "but there were plenty of times when I felt the same way. The dog loved to hunt and he was good in a duck marsh. But he was the *clumsiest* dog.

"If we were in a blind together, and I opened a Thermos and poured a cup of coffee, then it was for certain that Mose would decide that was the time to get up and turn around and spill my coffee. I don't know how many times he knocked the Thermos out of my hand, right when I was pouring the first cup of the day. One time, he hit it hard enough to knock it clean out of the blind. And the thing was, no matter how mad you were, no matter how much you wanted that hot coffee, there was always something funny about it."

Everyone agreed that there is something comically redeeming about a clumsy dog.

"Probably," the teller went on, "old Mose put on his greatest performance with somebody else in the blind. Friend of mine came down to hunt and he just fell in love with that dog. I tried to tell him the dog was a little bit . . . oh, *unpredictable*. But he wasn't having any. Said he and Mose would make an unbeatable team. So I dropped them off at one blind, in the dark, and went on around the marsh and set up in another blind. I was maybe two hundred yards away. I could hear my friend talking to Mose, telling him to 'sit' and 'stay.' Then it was quiet until the sun came up and the ducks came in.

"Now, Mose didn't cause any problems when the ducks were overhead. He was first class, that way. And after a couple of passes, six or seven mallards came into the decoys in front of my friend's blind. I heard him shoot. Heard the splash when the duck hit the water. Then I heard him say, kind of soft and confident, 'Okay, Mose. Fetch.'

"And then, the next thing I heard was him yelling like he'd been stabbed with a hot fork.

" 'No, Mose. No. *Whoa*, Mose.'

"But it was too late. I heard the dog hit the water. A little later, I heard my friend say, sort of soft and mournful, 'Oh, no.'

"I shouted across the marsh, kind of nervous, 'What happened?' "

" 'My *camera*,' my friend said.

"I figured Mose had knocked it off the ledge and into the mud, or something. So I hollered, 'How bad is it?'

" 'I don't know,' my friend said. 'I'll let you know when Mose gets back.'

"Now, at first I had a hard time figuring what he was talking about, but when he explained it later on, it all came clear. It seems that he'd carried this brand new, very expensive Nikon camera with a zoom lens to the blind in his bag. If I'd have seen it, I would have told him to leave it at home or get another dog.

"Anyway, when he got settled, he took the camera out of the bag and hung it from a peg, by the strap, so he could reach up and get it. Probably figured he was going to get a nice shot of Mose coming in with a retrieve.

"Well . . . what happened was, he downed that first duck and told Mose to fetch. Mose took off and put his head through the loop of that camera strap and kept right on going. Hit the water with that Nikon around his neck. Like I say, he was a good worker, so he just swam on out to where that mallard was floating and picked him up, then turned around and swam back in. Of course, my friend didn't have a camera when he *really* needed one. I'd have given anything for a picture of old Mose, coming out of the water with a drake mallard in his mouth and a Nikon camera hanging around his neck. My friend was laughing so hard he couldn't hunt. And it was his camera."

Everyone agreed that this was pretty good stuff. More to the point, nobody doubted the story. Of course the Lab had taken off out of the blind with a camera around its neck. That was *fated*, as the Greeks would have said, from the moment that fellow stepped into the duck blind carrying his camera.

Then one of the men, who had been silent up to this point, said, "I knew of a dog, one time, did something to top that."

Oh?

"Yeah, this dog was a chocolate Lab named Yoo Hoo, after the drink, you know. Anyway, Yoo Hoo was like most Labs. He was a good-timer and he just couldn't stand to be left alone. The fellow who owned him—name was Paul—was kind of a soft touch, and instead of leaving Yoo Hoo at home, by himself and sad, he'd let him ride around with him in his truck while he did his errands. The dog spent so much time in the truck that I believe Paul had him to where he could wear a seat belt and work the radio.

"Well, one day Paul has to go into town from the house, which is out on a country road, and he whistles up to Yoo Hoo and puts him in the shotgun seat. Paul gets in on the driver's side and starts down the driveway. It's about a quarter of a mile to the road, and halfway there, Paul remembers something.

"It's a narrow drive so he can't just turn around. And, since he doesn't want to back all the way to the house, he throws it in park and leaves Yoo Hoo in the truck, with the motor running, while he goes back to the house. Won't be but a minute, you see."

"Uh oh," one of the listeners said.

"Yeah, buddy," the narrator answered. "That was just too much opportunity for a Lab. And Paul made it worse by answering the phone and doing a couple of other things so he wound up spending fifteen or twenty minutes in the house. Then he walked out the front door, strolled down the driveway, and discovered that his truck was gone.

"Now, his first thought was that somebody had stolen his truck. Which was bad enough. But what made it worse was that the thief had also gotten Yoo Hoo. What's running through Paul's mind is that you can always get another truck, but he'll never be able to replace that Lab.

"He's standing there in the driveway, feeling terrible and just about to turn around and go back to the house and call the cops, when he hears something. The sound of an engine, down in the woods off the high bank where he built his driveway. He walks over and looks down into the woods. There is a clear set of tracks running, oh, about two hundred yards out into the woods, and at the end of the tracks, there is the pickup with Yoo Hoo at the wheel. Paul figured that the dog had spent so much time in the truck, watching him, that he knew about the gearshift and how it worked. He said that if the dog had just had an opposable thumb, he might have been able to get the truck down the driveway and gone on into town. Question was, what did he have in mind once he got there?"

• • •

I listened to all these stories, and more, and I enjoyed them. But I didn't have much to contribute. My dogs have come from the pointing breeds and they are the stoics. Some pointing dogs will work until they literally drop. They generally don't have the time for stunts. The comics come from among the retrievers. Especially Labradors. Since the day I sat and listened to those stories, I have met a Lab whose legend would hold up whenever the tales of great comic deeds are told. His name is Bernie.

He comes from Cleveland, and the breeder named him after the Brown's great quarterback, Bernie Kosar. The name fits the dog as perfectly as a stretch sock. You could never think of him as *Bernard*. He is a *Bernie* if ever there was one.

Bernie is a big yellow Lab with the kind of easy amiability that you see in a lot of big men. When you are big, you can come on gentle and nobody is likely to think it's because you are weak. I suppose Bernie can fight. I've seen him nicked up. But he is a party animal, not a fighter.

Bernie has a good nose and lots of drive. He is an excellent retriever both as a pickup dog off a mule wagon or out of a duck blind. But he seems to have sensed early in the game that he is not any better at this sort of basic, meat-and-potatoes dog work than a lot of other Labs. And Bernie wanted to be thought of as special. He was not content with a future that consisted of hundreds of competent, straightforward retrieves. Bringing duck after duck and quail after quail to the hand of a moderately grateful master in return for a few *Attaboys* was not the sort of vision to stir Bernie's soul. He was after bigger things, and like a starlet whose acting skills are no better than average but is determined to be a star, Bernie decided to make himself outrageous— to become a legend.

Nobody remembers Oscar Wilde for his poetry. Bernie is probably as good at sniffing out a freshly shot quail in the broomweed as Wilde was with verse. Maybe better. But an ordinary pickup doesn't really get Bernie's juices flowing, and sometimes he will get down off the wagon and run right past the spot where the bird has fallen. He will then proceed to run the country while the handler yells at him and the shooters mumble under their breath about ill-trained dogs, and the pointers, which are still on point, must be wondering why this bozo is allowed to get away with murder while they get whipped if they bust one lousy covey.

Bernie seems to know just exactly how long this sort of behavior will be tolerated before serious repercussions result. He does not want to be left in the kennel next time or whipped too hard this time. He'll take a whipping, but he's no masochist.

So, just when patience has been stretched to the breaking point, Bernie will suddenly remember what he has been sent out to do. He will make a straight line back to where the bobwhite fell, sniff around in the grass, make a show of picking up the scent and trailing—even if the bird fell stone dead and never moved an inch—then dash in the last ten feet and with the bird safely in his mouth, lift his head very high so everyone on the wagon or riding horseback can admire his form. Then, if this doesn't get results, Bernie will take a victory lap or two around the wagon before he brings the bird in to his handler.

A routine pickup is never really routine when Bernie is involved. He has a way of making the easy ones look hard.

Then, there are the hard ones. When Bernie has to trail a runner, he milks it for every ounce of drama. You'd think the bird was armed and dangerous. And of course, once the chase has ended, Bernie takes a victory lap.

On an unorthodox retrieve, he is even better. I watched him go after a runner that had gone down a gopher hole to hide; I consider it one of Bernie's finest moments. Bernie put his head into the gopher hole, then his feet, and then his entire body—until only his hindquarters were above ground. He moved close to a truckload of red clay to get at that bird.

"Seems like old Bernie would rather be a coal miner than a bird hunter," said one of the shooters, watching the show from the mule wagon.

"I just hope he doesn't find a rattlesnake down there," another shooter said.

At about that time, Bernie emerged from his excavations with the bird in his mouth. He got a round of applause from everyone on the wagon, and that just made his day.

While Bernie's technique is colorful, it is when he gets around water that his instinct for theater truly comes through.

Like most retrievers, Bernie quivers with anticipation when the ducks are coming in. In Bernie's case, I think it is something like stage fright. He knows he'll be on soon (provided the human does his rather humdrum part and shoots a duck or two), and for an artist, no matter how many times you have done it before, it is always opening night.

First thing that happens when a duck hits the water and a shooter says "fetch," is that Bernie *launches* himself like one of those NBA basketball players going for a dunk. Bernie milks his entry into the water for everything it's worth. Usually, this means the shooter is soaked. But this is a minor thing up against the making of a legend.

Occasionally, this big splash is enough to satisfy the performer in Bernie, and the remainder of the retrieve will follow the normal pattern. Bernie will swim out to the duck, pick it up in his mouth, swim back, and give the duck to the shooter. But this is no sure thing. It is not possible to know when the ham in Bernie will take over and he will decide that theatrics are called for.

This can take the form of something that might be called "Hide the Duck," which is pretty much what it sounds like. There is, however, no way to convey on paper and with mere words the kind of passions this seemingly harmless game can inspire. You wouldn't think grown men could be forced to such rhetorical heights by the actions of a mere dog. Bernie seems to think that the objective of this game is to get someone to go in over his waders, and about half the time, he is successful.

Bernie also likes another game that might be called "Where is the duck?" This game is best played when Bernie is taken to a blind and asked to retrieve a duck that he did not actually see fall. In those cases where the duck is floating out in the middle of open water, plainly visible to all, Bernie might just swim past it, so close that the duck is swamped by his wake. Hunters on shore will scream things like, *Right there, Bernie. Right there!*

Bernie will then begin to circle. First, the circles will grow wider. Then, as the screaming of the hunters grows louder and more shrill, the circles will grow tighter and tighter, with the duck in the precise center like the ten ring on a target. Finally, Bernie will locate the duck and return to shore in triumph.

A variation on this one occurs when the duck has fallen some-place where it can't be seen from shore. Say, in a patch of cattails. In a case like this, when Bernie is told to "fetch," he responds with a look and something like a shrug as though to say, "Fetch *what?*"

You can point as urgently as Napoleon directing his men through the Alps and Bernie will continue to give you the look. Finally, you decide to throw something out in the area where the duck has fallen. Then, of course, Bernie leaps into action. Big leap, lots of water splashed back on everyone on shore.

The basic comic script here calls for the dog to swim out and pick up the stick that the hunter has thrown to mark the duck. Bernie does this with the best of them. But he also seems to realize that this is pretty humdrum, pie-in-the-face sort of stuff. That what it needs is a *twist*.

Bernie has come up with a couple of variations on this theme and is, no doubt, working on others. The first variation calls for Bernie to swim right past the duck and even bump into it on his way to fetch the stick. He can do this with an absolutely straight face so that the hunter can believe that Bernie was actually unaware the duck was even there. Bernie's deadpan expression does not change even when three or four hunters scream, in unison, *Right there!*

A second, more elaborate variation calls for Bernie to swim out to where the stick has fallen close to the duck. He ignores the stick, picks up the duck, and turns back for the shore where the chorus is chanting *Good boy, thataway Bernie, bring him here.* About halfway to shore, Bernie drops the duck, turns around and picks up the stick, which he then brings to shore. It is as though Bernie wants everyone to understand that while he certainly knows the difference between a duck and a stick, he is not going to be locked into some rigid, orthodox thinking according to which a duck is *always* preferable to a stick. Some days, you see, he just feels more like retrieving sticks, even if there is a duck around.

It was on the day when I first saw this performance that I decided Bernie was interested, above all, in creating a legend. Now, while Bernie is certainly a ham, he is not necessarily a *prima donna*. He will jump—literally—at the opportunity to share the stage with other actors, though it is better if they are not dogs. He seems, in fact, to prefer beaver.

Take Bernie up to a quiet, concealed pond in the hour before dawn and everything will be fine—unless he hears the slap of a beaver tail. Then he is off. Swimming, diving, running, and barking. Just putting on a hell of a show that, in turn, inspires the beaver.

Usually beaver are pretty dour and phlegmatic. No time for fun and games as long as there is an undammed stream or an ungirdled aspen tree anywhere on the planet. But when Bernie comes around, beaver seem to turn into good-time-Charlies and hell-raisers with nothing to do but swim around the pond slapping the water with their tails. Near as I can tell, the game has a lot in common with tag, and Bernie is always "it." One thing is certain—no duck has ever been inclined to join in the fun, so on those mornings when Bernie and the beaver are at play, you have to be content to watch them and forget the hunt.

Bernie will also chase a deer or a turkey, and get close to a porcupine or a skunk. He is just naturally gregarious that way. He will run with just about anything that is alive and roll in just about anything that is dead. While he doesn't exactly play with insects, he will eat them. I've seen him wake up from a dead sleep to nail a grasshopper on the wing, which was not half as funny as the time he chomped down on a hornet that happened to fly by.

Bernie eats lots of interesting things, including some that were meant to be dinner. He has been thrown out of a lot of kitchens. Once, when he was inadvertently left in one where there was a ham on the counter, he managed to knock over a planter, open a faucet, and turn on a blender in his attempt (successful) to get at that meat. He spent several days in a maximum security kennel after that. Most dogs would have gotten life, but Bernie always seems able to wrangle a pardon.

Part of the reason is that he is always glad to see you. Genuinely glad. Bernie does not have to be called. If you are a kid, he is always ready to play. It would take three ten-year-olds, working in shifts, to wear him out. Kids have pulled his tail, stuck fingers in his eyes, and generally abused him, but he has never raised his voice or shown anyone his teeth. Bernie will go anywhere and do anything for kicks, so it doesn't seem so terrible if he can't be relied upon to stay with the script. He is an improviser and a clown. Aristotle, who could appreciate the Greek epics as well as anyone, wrote that man is the only animal that laughs. Which may be. I'm not going to argue with Aristotle.

But he never knew Bernie. And while I've never actually seen Bernie laugh, I know that he is a comic, and that if nothing else, he lives for the laughter of others. There is just no other way to account for him.

CHAPTER EIGHT

Knuckleheads and Wild Ringnecks
By E. Donnall Thomas, Jr.

There were dozens of places we could have hunted that day. The list of possibilities read like an encyclopedia of good pheasant cover: Conservation Reserve Program land bordering golden stubble fields, river bottoms lined with willows and chokecherries, uncultivated swales full of wild roses and native grasses that make you wonder how this country ever got by without pheasants before their introduction more than a hundred years ago. But the hunting season was reaching its middle age and the prairie lay in the grips of the first hard snow of the year. The birds were going to be stacked up in the middle of the nastiest, most impenetrable escape cover they could find—and I knew just the place to look for them.

When I called the night before to confirm my invitation to hunt his land, the rancher, a longtime friend, warned me that it had been a wet year; the cover was high and thick, and the creek bottoms we planned to hunt still held water. One or two other local hunters had been out earlier, but they had been unable to move many birds from the heavy cover. Ray and I remained unde-terred as we finalized our plans over coffee. We could have pre-dicted everything the rancher had told me anyway. His place has always held a special appeal during the late season: I imagined how the frost-brittle cattails in the creek bottom would feel and what the flushing roosters would sound like as they fought their way through them toward the sky. There might be easier places to hunt, but today, I wouldn't miss this one for the world.

During the hour's drive from my house to the ranch, the coun-tryside around us seemed stunned, as if it was not yet ready for the changing of the seasons. The puddle ducks that had dotted the stock ponds a few days earlier were gone, and the antelope along the roadside stood and stared indifferently as if they were preoccupied with the threat of winter. Finally, we turned off the county road and eased down a rutted two-track; and there was the creek bottom, as devilish and defiant a patch of late-season pheasant cover as one could imagine.

Ray and I stopped at our customary parking spot and opened the dog box in the back of the truck; our retrievers spilled forth, uncontainably excited. The dry snow exploded beneath their feet and hung shimmering in the sunlight as they roared around and jumped up on us enthusiastically, displaying just the sort of canine bad manners that never seem to bother me as much as I know they're supposed to. They were our secret weapons, the reason I never pay any attention when well-meaning landowners tell me that the birds have been tough lately. All the dogs wanted now was to hunt, a desire that made perfect sense to me.

As I sat down on the tailgate of the truck and struggled into my hip waders, one foot brushed against the ground by accident and contaminated my wool sock with snow. That is just the sort of trivial mishap that can aggravate you all day long. The rubber boots felt stiff and confining, and I tried to talk myself right back out of them, but the voice of my own experience prevailed. I knew what was waiting down in the creek bottom, and the desire to hunt in leather boots wasn't going to make the footing any drier. The cold shudder of snow in my left boot made me grimace as I stood, but finally there was nothing to do but reach for my game vest and go hunting.

After walking easily across two hundred yards of stubble, climbing down into the creek bottom felt like a descent into hell. The artificial civility of cultivation yielded at once to a murderous tangle of brush, beaver workings, and thorns in a dozen different shapes and sizes, as if all the flora there had been designed to protect the place against intrusion. Along the bottom of the draw, the partly frozen creek expanded and contracted according to the whim of the beavers. The ice was too thick to walk through and too thin to walk on, and treacherous sinkholes were everywhere. It was simply no place for right-thinking people. No wonder the pheasants love it there.

Our routine felt easy and familiar. One of us would take the dogs through the brush toward the apex of each curve in the creek while the other waited where the water pushed against the high bank at the outside of the bend. As the two dogs worked their way through these naturally defined segments of cover, the creek closed relentlessly on the birds running in front of them, until they had no choice but to flush. Each of us knew just where to go and just what to do without having to discuss it—our dogs were both veterans at this exercise.

The first bend produced a handful of hens and a lone rooster for Ray. I was the blocker on the second push, and doubled easily on the pair of ringnecks that the dogs flushed over my head. The next stretch of cover, an isolated oxbow, proved to be the honey hole. I completed my limit on a noisy rooster that tried to cut behind me, while Ray quickly managed an overhead double of his own. For another minute, the dogs worked pheasants against the oxbow's outside bank and nosed them into the air, until we finally collected our canine partners and sent them on the retrieves they were bred for.

"You know," Ray said, as we hauled ourselves up out of the creek bottom and started back across the field toward the truck, "we could have hunted here all morning without seeing a bird if it hadn't been for the knuckleheads."

I mumbled in agreement and reached down to pull a cluster of burrs from my wool pants. The weight of the birds in the game vest felt like an apology for the creek bottom's uncivil manners. I remembered my rancher friend and the pessimism he'd expressed, and imagined earlier hunters nibbling around the edges of the cover without benefit of experienced dogs. Beside me, my Lab was staring longingly back toward the creek as if he were sorry to have the morning end so soon.

• • •

While I have great respect for the pointing breeds, I remain a hopeless aficionado of the Labrador retriever. I love Labs—don't ask me to explain. We just seem to understand each other and to approach the world with a fundamentally similar set of priorities, an admission with which certain co-workers and an ex-wife would no doubt agree. Because I make it a point to live in places where I can hunt a lot, my kennel has to be productive. It also has to be versatile, since any given day here on the prairie might provide the opportunity to hunt everything from Hungarian partridge to geese. Sure, I could have Labs *and* more traditional upland bird dogs—but every place in my kennel occupied by something other than a Lab would be, well, one less Lab in my life. As I said, don't ask for explanations.

These circumstances have led me to accumulate more than my share of experience with flushing retrievers, dogs that have never enjoyed the reputation they deserve in sophisticated wingshooting circles. They are all too often dismissed as dogs that couldn't make it by "real" retriever standards, or as an unsophisticated hunter's poor substitute for a properly trained pointer.

Part of the problem is historical. Flushing retrievers don't really come into their own as upland bird dogs unless they are hunting pheasants. By the time pheasants were firmly established in the West, Labs had years of waterfowling tradition behind them. Virtually everything official concerning these popular dogs ignored their utility as upland gun dogs—everything, that is, except an appreciation of their versatility by the people who love to hunt with them.

Flushing Labradors demand their own approach to hunting upland game. Part of the problem is that a good many people just don't get it, especially those who have spent their days afield in the company of pointing breeds. A dog that flushes birds generally does little good unless the blessed event takes place within shotgun range, a need that can be addressed in different ways. You might learn to run faster than the dog, in which case you should stop wasting time in hunting boots and begin to train seriously for the Olympics. You can avoid hunting wild pheasants, an option that concedes the battle before it starts. Or, you can use the one organ that is supposed to work better in people than it does in dogs or pheasants—the brain.

Pheasants rise in front of flushing dogs either because they have made a mental error or because they have exhausted their possibilities on the ground. Unless you enjoy running wind sprints against competition that will always be faster than you, establishing yourself at the end of a limiting terrain feature with the dog working the birds toward you is one way to make optimal use of a flushing Labrador's ability. The essential skill is being able to anticipate what pheasants will do when pressured and where they will eventually flush.

Teamwork is critical to success in the flushing retriever game, and such teamwork involves hunters and dogs alike. While I enjoy hunting alone, I do appreciate the presence of an experienced hunting partner when I'm working educated ringnecks. This is especially true of the two or three people I hunt with regularly. Working a stretch of cover in such company often becomes a series of back-and-forth drives in miniature, a style that takes the fullest advantage of the things flushing Labradors do best.

It is important to realize that the qualities that make great non-slip retrievers do not necessarily make great flushing dogs. In a duck blind, the hunter controls the pace of the hunt, and style on the part of the dog boils down to how tightly innate canine energy can be focused on the intentions of the hunter. In upland bird work, on the other hand, it is the dog that often determines the hunt's tempo, and individual qualities of initiative and intelligence become irreplaceable.

• • •

It is the last day of a long upland bird season. The leaden sky sits heavily on the prairie and the sun is nothing but a dull, indistinct presence above the distant southern horizon. I am alone except for my dog, Sonny—a state of affairs that seems to capture the mood of the day perfectly.

After two months of hunting, the easy birds are gone, and those that remain are fluent in the art of survival. They are all holed-up now, in the thickest of the CRP, the most horrendous cattail tangles, and here, in a coulee so choked with thorn apple and buffalo berry that even the range cattle can't get through it. With all due respect for the pointing breeds, this is no place for a dog that looks as if it should be posing for a picture on a calendar. This is knucklehead country.

An earthen dam's bare shoulders rise above the cover a quarter of a mile in front of us. There might still be some open water behind it, but the possibility of jumping a mallard invokes all

71

sorts of lead shot–steel shot legal complications, so I ignore it. Besides, waterfowl season goes on for two more weeks, but the stretch of cover below the dam promises to hold the last pheasants of the year.

The dog knows what to do. He is hunting smart now. His occasional early season reversions to puppyhood have been tempered by weeks' worth of cagey ringnecks. He follows quietly to the lip of the coulee, but when I send him down the bank, he hits the cover with absolute abandon. This is an old, familiar game for both of us. If I were to go down into the brush with him, I would never be able to see enough to shoot. If I paralleled his course on the edge of the cover, the birds would simply flush from the other side, out of range. But we have other things in mind.

With the dog all but lost to the cover, I cut across a bend in the coulee and position myself on the dam. There are a dozen mallards tucked behind it in a splash of open water the size of my kitchen table; I stand at port arms and watch them rise into the winter sky with an ambivalent sense of regret.

Now I can see Sonny cross an opening in the heavy cover a hundred yards away, tail alive, nose to the ground, his attention perfectly focused upon the unseen vector of a running bird known only by its scent. My hands close reflexively on the familiar weight of the double, and then the first of the birds reach the dam and the end of the cover. A pair of hens flush to my left, then a rooster is right in my face, cackling angrily before folding at the shot. There follows a chaotic minute of pheasants, shooting, and dog work as I pick two more cocks from the riot in progress. Then there is nothing to do but enjoy the retrieves, scratch Sonny's ears, turn my back on another bird season, and walk on off into what's left of the year.

• • •

I have friends who just don't understand. They cannot imagine why I live in upland bird country without a kennel full of stylish pointers. When I take them bird hunting, they wonder why I always seem to be where the birds are getting up. They question the lung-straining pace of the pursuit and shake their heads at what seems more like chaos than strategy. Wouldn't it be easier, they are always asking, if I got myself a pointing dog and saved those crazy Labs for the ducks?

I won't argue about what might be easier. I will not even point out that these questions are often asked over a dinner of pheasants that would never have arrived at the table had we spent the day hunting with dogs other than my own.

I will argue, however, that the flushing Labrador is capable of giving something special where it counts. When you have watched your dog outwit a particularly wily rooster in a way made possible only by years of teamwork in the field, the retrieve and the weight of the bird in your hand and the taste of the pheasant dinner that follows can become their own measures of style.

CHAPTER NINE

The Cartway of Time
By Ted Nelson Lundrigan

Time passes in one direction only. Its door swings open and things go through it, but a man cannot return across any threshold except his own. All that remains of the pasts of others are the things they left behind.

There is the foundation of a grand house built into a hillside just downstream from the Pedersen farm pond. Facing south, its remains are a Stonehenge collection of poured concrete walls and window openings. The wood for a dwelling of this size was not cut from those waist-high stumps above the beaver dam. It was milled in town and hauled out here, where it was formed into a fine frame house with a spacious porch from which its owners could enjoy the view of the valley and its tumbling brook. A great meadow must have stretched out from the streambank, rising to meet the woods' edge that crested the high ridge. I know this because the trees all along the ridge are old oaks, but those from the oaks back to the brook and up to the ruins are younger trees and almost all poplar.

That is how my Labrador, Dixie, and I found this homesite

and the old road. When I say "old road," I am not referring to it in the sense of time. What I mean is the way it came to be formed by the hills and streams that it was made to cross. When the township supervisors got enough money, they abandoned it for the "new" road, which is now a grass-centered mud-rut trail right down the section line.

"One day is one mile." That was the township rule in those days. The Caterpillar that made it was a big one with an engine that could only be started by putting a crowbar into its flywheel hole and yanking the crankshaft over until it caught hold with a cough and roar. Then it was four passes after the trees were cut: one down each side to lay the earth to the middle, and one more on each side to crown it up. The road was made along the town line to the corner that is now my landmark to turn and park next to the old wrecked tractor, a Minneapolis Moline in its younger and better days.

A cartway is one rod wide, sixteen and one-half feet. There were a lot of them in the early days of this land. They were the trails that connected one homestead to another, and they wound between the hills or around them when necessary. A cartway was part road and part game trail. When it came to a stream, a crossing called a low-water ford was constructed. Most of these were built by the timber companies to pull the logs out to the mill landings. The farmers and settlers adopted them as the easiest way to travel through the country. Neither the deer nor the teamsters went out of their way to cut through a hill just to keep a straight line.

• • •

I had flushed a bird from the weedy ditch of the town road on my way to the turnoff. The area was then unfamiliar to me, and when that is so, it is my practice to follow birds. What better guide to new grouse hunting than a native? The bird had flown into a cluster of poplar sprouts that formed the edge of a grassy opening. I parked the old car, shrugged on my vest, and turned out Dixie. The edge turned downhill, and from this vantage I could see spread out before me the lower reaches of a flooded meadow and the high oak crest of the ridge that turned the flow of Wood Row Creek.

About midway down the hill was a copse of old pines and some newer trees gathered in one spot. On the right of this, glowing in the sun, were two bright red apples. A singular sight for Minnesota, and especially so in late October. The grouse was now forgotten for a crisp red apple on a golden fall afternoon. I ate one, put the other in my pocket, and threw the core to the dog. Next to me, Dixie loved two other things in all the world: the first was retrieving; the second was eating anything that did not eat her. These were big apples and it was an old tree. With visions of eastern grouse shooting in my head, I explored around the nearby corners and niches.

A fire had consumed the wooden parts of the house and had, probably at the same time, opened the hard-sealed cones of the nearby pines, because their small grove was in reality the basement or root cellar of the home. I walked around in front of these, and there facing the valley were four tablets of cement. They were window openings without the wood cap at the top. Tombstones for a house now crumbled into its own grave.

In the meantime, Dixie had been busy scuffling and snuffling after the bird. A whir of wings made me turn around in time to watch the grouse sail downhill. It turned sharp right to fly into an archway in the trees.

I kept my eyes fixed on that spot and walked quickly toward the woods' edge. The grass was high. I stepped into a small ditch in the same way, and with the same grace, that one misses the last step in a staircase.

I was standing on an old roadbed. It started at the hilltop, curved past the dooryard of the home, and disappeared in the dim light of the arch, traveling down to a small creek that ran into the larger flow of the little river. I walked down the raised portion of the trail, my stomach twisting with the pleasant tightness that occurs in anticipation of a new adventure.

The heavy field grass couldn't live in the shade of this place, but the ferns could. The frost had taken them down and spread the fronds out in a carpet of dark brown stretching across the lane from one old ditch to the other. About midway between myself and the far mud bank of the little tributary, a black log lay across the trail. Dixie snuffled and scuffed through the dry debris until she was standing in the creek. She walked along in the water, lapping up its flow, swinging her tail happily from side to side.

Among her other fine qualities, Dixie had a very expressive face. There is always some speculation in giving human qualities to dog behavior, but I think that an animal can express surprise as well as any man. Dixie jerked her head up and at the same time raised her eyebrows with a grunt. There, on the creek bank, stood a grouse snapping its tail open and shut in agitated display. She was never much of a bird-watcher. In about the time it took her to draw in the required breath, she was bursting out of the water in pursuit.

The grouse was up off the ground, grabbing for the air between the dog and the overstory of ash trees. Straight up it climbed, and I followed its flight with the swing of my shotgun until the barrels went past its head. I shot, but the bird just staggered for a slight drop, then it surged up again, reaching higher and higher for the space above those shadows on the ground. I followed it and pressed the back trigger. The recoil of the gun carried my leading hand past the climbing grouse in a gesture as if to say: "After you, Alfonse."

He stalled, and in a perfect Immelmann turned on his wing to bank back toward the ground. He must have died at about that moment, for he lost all control and, spinning in a slow spiral, fell into the treetops. From there he bounced from limb to limb until, disdaining all contact with the ground, he hung himself in the crotch of a branch, swinging back and forth beyond the reach of the dog.

"This one would have smoked the last cigarette to a stub and spit at the firing squad, Dixie." I slipped the bird into my game pocket. "Let's follow this old road and see if he has any brothers."

The rivulet was hardly more than a short hop to the other bank, but it had patiently worked its will on the roadbed until the cut was deep enough to let the water into the main flow of Wood Row Creek. The homesteader had raised enough earth to allow me to climb out of the little valley and along the side of the main ridge. Here the beaver had done their work, clearing the trees to build the big dam now in sight upstream. The gray dogwood bushes had filled in the sunlit opening from the tributary's valley to the dam. Great trees blocked my way, felled by the beavers but too big to drag into the water. I climbed up on one trunk in order to step over to another, and in this manner made my way toward the little opening where the tractor lay. From time to time a grouse was flushed by Dixie, who was out somewhere ahead of me but invisible in the underbrush. There was no chance for a shot, for I was always out of balance or under an overhang. Finally, panting for a breath and swearing revenge against the clan, I rested on the steel saddle of the old tractor.

There are the ruins of a deer shack in a spruce grove close by. Another man's land cuts into the long edge of the Pedersen holding, not unlike a brick in a staggered wall. The very corner of the tract is adjacent to the tractor, and it was here the cabin was built, close to water and the road. Because of its proximity to the road, the little house was vandalized and its walls torn out. Within a few years the rest of the front collapsed into the basement hole and it became a haven for porcupines, bears, and the like.

If the birds flew straight along the creek they might have settled near the old ruins. So, with that in mind, I sent the dog on ahead and took the path that would bring me past the open end. She seemed awfully interested in the part that was collapsed in front. Her tail was wagging furiously as she pawed and whined to find a way in.

I stepped up quickly, grabbing her collar to keep her away from what I assumed was a skunk or a prickly tail. It was neither polecat nor porcupine. Inside the ruins, walking about on the floor, were three grouse.

The first to start upright was the nearest bird. In the next second it was flying straight up through the hole in the cabin roof like a feathered bottle rocket. This startled the other two and they split in two directions, one out the broken window, and the other out the door, passing close enough to touch my nose with its wingtip.

I was already somewhat off balance trying to stand bolt upright with a seventy-pound Lab in my hand, and I was dumped on my backside when Dixie seized the opportunity to lunge at the bird closest to my face.

Some years later I would relate this story to Arthur Pedersen, who responded in his Norwegian brogue: "Vell, you know dat der is two tin plates in dat front vindow of our house? Yah, und I come up to dat vindow ven der was only one pane broke, und I say, Vut is dis? I look in dat window und der in duh house is a pat'ridge. He is valking here and der. Und he sees me. Und he takes uff right thru anutter vindow. You tink he would use dah same vun. Yah, sure."

Arthur was speaking of the second house, which was built around 1920. The first one was on a hilltop near the creek. The same cartway that I was tracing through the lowland wound its way close to the deer shack ruins, through a small pasture, past the site of that second house, and close to the big barn, then turned along the edge of the hill to find its way to the foot of what is now an enormous white pine. Here, there was a bridge built on rock pilings. It is all gone now, but when my Lab, Dixie, and I first found it, the planks were still there.

On the far side of the bridge the roadbed is soft with the remains of old corduroy logs and a dense alder run leaning over the sides to shade out the sun. It is a heavy, wet, slippery jungle of vines and leaves. This is the home of the Bridge Bird . . .

CHAPTER TEN

The Retriever Game
By Boyd Gibbons

To the skeptical reader desiring credentials, here's my badge: I have competed in a field trial. Actually, it was one test. And the trial was informal. Okay, so it wasn't much of a retrieve, either. My dog and I provided entertainment for the gallery, but I can't say that our foray to the line attracted further invitations.

It happened this way. Some years ago, wanting to learn how to get my first Lab—a pup named Ben, no initials—beyond mere obedience and into reliable retrieving, I sought out advice. This led me to a small sign at the edge of a road on the Eastern Shore. The sign read: FIELD TRIAL. I turned off the highway and followed a succession of arrows through the woods and out to a fan of trucks and station wagons parked at the edge of an immense stubble field of corn. People were walking about with whistles hanging from their necks and dogs at their sides. I got Ben out of his crate, snapped on his lead, and attempted an impression of a retriever person.

If pride goeth before a fall, mine certainly wenteth. The bait was placed by the sort of casual inquiry that field trialers use to smoke out the weekend klutz.

"Does your dog retrieve?"

The jig was up. As a retriever person, I was hardly to the larval stage. Did Ben retrieve? From the woodpile he distributed splits of oak around the yard. He retrieved our socks, our shoes, our houseguests' embarrassments. Until Ben, my experience with dogs had been limited to an Irish setter so delinquently bonkers that my grandfather had forbidden his presence on hunts, and a dachshund that defied mortality and peed on the rug. Ben would be different. Ben would be obedient, he would hunt. Ben would do calculus.

"Does my dog retrieve? Sure."

The derby stake was for young dogs, so I entered him. My wife was of the opinion that I had taken leave of reality. Having no idea what I was supposed to do, I watched the other dogs retrieve. The test was a single mark, if you can describe as a mark a dead pigeon thrown by a tiny figure that appeared to be at least a mile away. It was evident that I was in a serious poolroom with deadly shooters. The other dogs may as well have had names like Vinny and Killer. They leaned against lampposts and spit in the gutter. They were lean, aggressive rockets, about as soft as gneiss. If these were pups, I was Mahatma Ghandi.

When Ben's name was announced, I walked him to the line and said, *Sit.* Slowly Ben sat. He looked up at me in all his puppy softness. This was ridiculous. In a sympathetic voice that implied it would be no disgrace to back out now, the judge asked if I was ready, and for reasons inexplicable to the sensible mind what came out of my mouth was, "Yes!" At that distance the gun made a sound like *pap*, and an object the size of a pea fell somewhere in the largest field in North America.

I said, "Fetch!"

Ben trotted out about fifteen feet and began making circling moves indicating that he was about to do some marking of a different sort. The judge yelled to the guns, "Help him out!" The guns yelled, "Hey, hey, hey!" Ben galloped out maybe fifty feet, went into his disengaged mode, squatted; the guns yelled *heyheyheyheyhey*, he ran some more, reconsidered, stopped to examine a corncob, peed on a dirt clod. He eventually reached the rough proximity of the guns, where he piddled around for what seemed like the better part of the afternoon until he stumbled upon the dead pigeon. He did some investigative sniffing. He picked up the bird by the tip of its wing as though it were a claymore mine.

I began yelling victoriously, right through the rulebook. "Ben! Ben, come! Come! Come ON! COME ON, FELLA! COME ON, BEN, THAT'S THE STUFF, BOY, *COME ON!*" Dog trainers advise commands of brevity. I was working my way into an essay. But I'll be go-to-hell, he had the damned pigeon and he was bringing it right to me! I considered the possibilities of a press conference, where I would accept the trophy, the accolades, while, of course, appearing modest before the cameras as I gave advice to the handlers huddled at my feet.

Ben galloped by me in triumph, past the judges and the

gallery, and into the woods, where he proceeded to eat the pigeon.

I went home and bought James Lamb Free's *Training Your Retriever*. I also bought a retrieving bumper, which looked like a salami of squeezable plastic, and tied on a short throwing rope. Free described the "Baseball Diamond Method of Teaching Hand Signals." He said to imagine a baseball diamond. I took his advice literally. I walked Ben to a nearby school and sat him on the pitcher's mound. Following Free's instructions, I threw the bumper toward second, left Ben on the mound, and returned to home plate. I raised my arm and yelled, *Back!* In time, I extended these casts to the right (first base) and left (third base).

If trained often enough, Free wrote, you can eventually hide the bumpers and the dog will go on the command alone. Which Ben did—when it suited him, or when there was compelling evidence (the honking above the blind, the gunfire) that there was warm goose out on the river.

Despite my limited talents, Ben was an eager hunter and dependable retriever. But his enthusiasm for blind retrieves could be measured by the stones I threw in the direction of downed birds. And he considered steadiness to be an academic exercise. When the grouse and the guns went off in the opaque thickets of West Virginia, Ben took off as well, in whatever direction inspired him. *Steady to Wing and Shot* was not on his license plate.

In searching for another pup during Ben's declining years, I was drawn to a number of weekend field trials and eventually the 1988 National in Oklahoma. If I saw retrievers at the line bounce like yo-yos, there were also retrievers steady as oaks that marked

and remembered the falls of numerous birds at distances requir-
ing magnification by Zeiss, that went from a dead run to statuary
at the sound of the whistle, that took any variety of casts to God
knows where and retrieved with a firm but gentle mouth. I saw
dogs do all that with style and eagerness, then sit stoically by
and honor another dog as the birds went up and the honored
dog went out.

This wasn't my game, but I enjoyed the moves and I wanted
to learn more about it.

• • •

In the brains of dogs there resides an irresistible urge to chase
down prey. Terriers prefer mice and rats, greyhounds course
rabbits, and a cat seems to raise the level of adrenaline in them
all. This has not been lost on generations of hunters, who have
channeled that instinct in the sporting breeds into the pursuit of
game birds for the table.

As dogs are the elaborate extensions of their owners' egos, it
was only a matter of time until a group of Englishmen decided in
1865 to see who had the best hunting dog by testing them in
competition in the field.

About that time in Tennessee a man by the name of P. H.
Bryson, who had been shot up in the Civil War and sent home
to become a statistic, received some encouraging advice from
his physician: Buy yourself a shotgun and a bird dog and go
hunting. In the South a bird dog meant one of the pointing
breeds—wide-ranging pointers and setters—which, until the Lab
got its substantial toehold on this continent in the 1930s, were the

American hunting dogs of choice. Bryson bought a setter and went after quail.

In 1874, his body intact and his enthusiasm for hunting dogs still rising, he organized, near Memphis, the first field trial in the United States, restricted, understandably enough, to setters and pointers. Retriever competitions did not begin in the United States for more than another half-century.

Of the eighty-two National and National Amateur Retriever Championships held since 1941 and 1957, all but five have been won by Labrador retrievers. Golden retrievers have won only one National Amateur and four Nationals. No Chesapeake Bay retriever has won either.

Why this is so is a subject that divides breeders and trainers as much as it does the dogs. Some say that the sensitive golden is too much of a lover, the Chessie too independent. Few Chessies show up at retriever field trials; some Goldens will be in the running; but the reigning dog is the one with the brown eyes and the slick black (or yellow) coat; the versatile, driving Labrador retriever.

Hamilton Rowan, longtime director of field trials for the American Kennel Club, believes that the Labrador has dominated retriever trials because it can endure the punishment of the training. "A golden can't take that kind of training, nor a Chessie. You keep firing electricity into a Chessie and he's going to come back and take your hand off. It isn't that the Lab is a better dog—he just has a different temperament and can take it. Of course, a Lab person would hang you from a tree if you said that to him."

Rex Carr, who has probably trained more National and National Amateur retriever champions than anyone, is prepared to get out the rope. "The principal difference between retriever breeds is not as Hamilton Rowan expressed it. Labradors haven't dominated field trials because they can take the punishment of training—it's because of their retrieving instinct and desire."

From the early nineteenth century, the Labrador's breeding was managed by the British aristocracy, who had the time, money, and influence to develop a superior retriever. By the turn of the twentieth century, the Labrador retriever had become the preferred dog at shoots in England and Scotland. Today, when retrievers go to trial across the kale and beet fields of England, it is no surprise that the Labs of Sandringham House have a place at the line. The kennels at Sandringham House are the kennels of the Queen of England.

An attraction for things British led Americans of influence who had hunted over Labs on driven grouse shoots in Scotland to bring these dogs back with them to their Long Island estates. They brought, as well, Scottish gamekeepers to raise ducks and pheasants for the shoots and to train and handle the dogs.

In 1931, the Labrador Retriever Club helped organize the first retriever field trial in the United States. It was held at *Glenmere Court*, Chester, New York: eight thousand acres of marsh and field and pen-raised pheasants. Licensed by the AKC, the event was run in the manner of the early English trials, with an advancing line of beaters, three guns with attendants, and two handlers with their dogs at heel. Boys in the ditches threw live pheasants into flight. Guns came to shoulders. The judge directed which dog would make the retrieve. The trial took place on December 21, not because it was on the eve of winter but because it fell on a Monday. There was a strong interest among the sponsors not to attract common spectators to the gallery.

The early years of retriever field trials were Long Island social events draped with Loden and tweed. There were boots by Gokey, by Russell, high-laced English boots. Burberry bi-swing shooting coats with bellows pockets. Barbour rain gear of Egyptian long-staple cotton that had been boiled in vats of oil and wax. There were wool knickers, gabardine jodhpurs, English cavalry twill and whipcord trousers faced in calfskin, Viyella shirts, silk English ascots, and slouch hats and snap brims so loaded down with trial and club pins it's a wonder the felt didn't collapse.

The competition was loose. Handlers threw stones into the water to show the dogs the duck. A two-stone retrieve beat a three-stone retrieve. As so few dogs were competing, the trial had an intermission for a leisurely lunch. The National Champion was simply the retriever who had accumulated the most points that year at field trials, of which there were a few—five in 1935, ten in 1937, twenty in 1940. The idea of a conclusive annual trial to determine the top retriever did not bear fruit until 1941, when the National Retriever Field Trial Club was formed to run the National Championship Stake. Only fifteen retrievers ran in the first National at Penniman's Point, Quogue, Long Island. The trial was over in three days, concluding on the Sunday that Pearl Harbor came under attack.

By the 1988 National in Oklahoma, the field trial game had progressed some distance beyond one-stone retrieves. So many retrievers were competing—eighty-five in all—that the contest ran from before dawn to dusk, Monday through Saturday, opening in Indian summer and finishing in a winter storm. More than time and distance separated this National from the social strata of prewar Long Island. Out on range land unburdened by the italics of grand estate names, the handlers were the core of a small, insular society of tenaciously competitive trialers and their muscular, athletic dogs. Times had changed, and the trialers and their dogs had shifted with the years.

CHAPTER ELEVEN

King Buck
By Richard A. Wolters

[Editor's Note: King Buck, a Labrador retriever, is considered by most authorities to be one of the finest—if not the finest—Labs ever whelped. From 1952 through 1957, he dominated the national field trial circuit and, at the same time, became a superb wild duck retriever. Buck was owned, primarily, by John Olin of Winchester Arms and Nilo Kennels, and was trained by the legendary Cotton Pershall. This is King Buck's story.]

John Olin recalls that "King Buck was the greatest Labrador I've seen anywhere. The dog seemed to have almost human brains. When the going got tough, he got tougher; it was just unbelievable. That dog really was a part of me before we parted company with his death. I never had a dog that had so much affection in him. He was a real crowd-pleaser.

"The National down in Maryland, which we won in '53, was the most exciting trial I've ever seen. The dog had the trial won up to the ninth series, then he had to be handled; he mismarked a bird and Cotton Pershall had to handle him. He went through the tenth series and did a perfect job, and they declared the two extra series. The eleventh series was a tough one. It was a triple mark and then a blind through a cut out to a bay with a duck attached to a float, with waves and irregular shoreline. The bay was in a fit with good strong winds and waves. Buck nailed the three marks on the blind, he took a line, went right through the middle of that cut, and went directly to that duck with no whistle. I remember Dan Pomeroy and I were sitting in an old chicken coop watching. When I saw Buck pick up that duck I almost hollered, 'Man, here it is, we've got it. There will be no other dog that will perform this, and if any does, it will be with a whistle.' That's just what happened; they had to hack the dog all the way. Buck did it without a single whistle!"

King Buck and Cotton Pershall were destined to be a team; they both had the same birthday. Cotton wasn't born in duck country, but King Buck was—one of a litter of eight, born in 1948 at Storm Lake in northwest Iowa. Timothy of Arden was the sire, owned by Ed Quinn. The dam, Alta of Banchory, had five males and three females. There was nothing spectacular about the pups, and they all received their early training from Quinn. They took to water like Lab pups usually do and showed early promise as good gun dogs. At six months of age they were all sold, and when it got down to the last two, of which King Buck was one, the price was down to $50. These were sent to their new owners in Omaha and on arrival both came down with distemper. One of the pups didn't make it. Robert Howard took his pup home and placed it in a basket next to the basement furnace.

The little retriever showed no improvement, and Howard was advised several times to have him put to sleep. For nearly a month the pup was as sick as an animal can be and remain living. But Mrs. Howard's loving attention and devotion to the sick puppy finally turned the battle.

One night Bob Howard went downstairs to have a look at him. The pup managed to stand in his basket and greet him. He knew then that he was going to make it.

Yet the effects of distemper weren't shaken off overnight. King Buck did not eat well and was very thin. When Howard took the young dog to a veterinarian, he was told that Buck had a bad heart and should not be run in the field. As if this weren't bad enough, the dog's stools were sometimes bloody, and Howard feared that his Lab might have suffered internal damage. Yet, Buck ran well. Even more important, he wanted to run. And by the time he was eighteen months old, his weight and appetite began to improve and Howard never noticed symptoms of poor health again.

In his second autumn the dog began his first field hunting. A very brainy dog, Buck was also eager and affectionate and showed no inclination of being shy or a one-man dog. He did not suddenly "come of age" as some dogs do. He won a licensed derby when he was only eighteen months old. The young dog also won first place in September, 1949, at the Missouri Valley Hunt Club's licensed trial in Iowa.

By this time, Howard sensed a quality of greatness in the young Labrador. He wanted to give Buck a real chance to prove himself but could not afford to run his retriever in top-flight trials. So he sold King Buck to Byron "Bing" Grunwald of Omaha for $500, with the stipulation that Howard would continue to train the Labrador and handle him in trials.

Bing Grunwald, who started in field trials in 1946 and was president of the National Amateur Club in 1961 and the National Open Club in 1964, picks up the story from there.

"In November of 1949 Bob Howard came to me and said, 'You know my first wife passed away with cancer; I remarried. This girl's name is Mildred; she's doing a fine job taking care of my two girls and now we're going to have one of our own. I would like to sell you King Buck for $500 and use the $500 to buy Mildred a special Christmas present.' I said, 'I'll just give you the $500,' and I wrote him a check. He said, 'There's a catch to this. I think this dog is going to be outstanding. I would like to train the dog until he's three years of age.' I said, 'Well, keep the check.' So that's the way I bought King Buck. I am bragging when I say I bought King Buck out of the kindness of my heart to help this man buy his wife a Christmas present; no one knew that he was going to be what he turned out to be.

"When the dog was three years of age we ran him in April 1951 in a licensed trial in Lincoln, Nebraska, and Bob Howard lost him on a land blind. I attended the trial and he came to me and said, 'Bing, you have done everything that you agreed to do. This dog has turned out to be a fine animal. You should give him to a big-time trainer and go in with him because he's going to produce good results. I think the number one trainer in the U.S. is Cotton Pershall.' I told him, 'If you can get Friday off we'll drive up to the trial at Eagle, Wisconsin, and take it in and talk to Cotton.' I found out when I got there that Cotton Pershall had just gone to work for John Olin, so that limited him training for me.

"We ran the trial Saturday and Sunday. King Buck ran six series and won the trial. The first thing that happened was a man named Snuffy Beleveau, an old-time professional, came to my wife and offered me $4,000 for King Buck. That was the first offer that we had. As soon as we got back home the telephone started ringing; everybody wanted to buy the dog. A man named Mr. Kline, who won the National Open in 1956, offered me $7,500; Paul Bakewell called and offered to send me the best brood bitch in America and a check for $5,000 for Buck. I would breed the brood bitch, keep and raise all the puppies, and send the brood bitch back to him—so this was a fine offer. I just debated about it and kept thinking about Cotton Pershall. So finally a friend of mine by the name of Arthur Stores called; he had just returned from fishing with Mr. John Olin. He said, 'What are you going to do with that dog?' 'Well,' I said, 'I've had a lot of offers, but I would like to see Cotton Pershall get the dog. If they buy him, I'll take $6,500 and two male puppies from his breeding.' 'Well,' he said, 'that's a lot of money.' I said, 'I've been offered $7,500, and I have been offered this other deal, but not for that much.' He said, 'Let me call you back.'

"In forty-five minutes he called me, and Mr. Olin bought the dog. He said he was going to change his name to Gold Dust because they couldn't imagine that any dog should be worth $6,500. Mr. Olin was just opening his Nilo Kennels for field trials, so it was brand new to him. So now John Olin got the dog. Of the two puppies I received, I gave one to a friend and both of us gave them away when they were twelve months of age because they would not retrieve. King Buck was never a sire of good field trial dogs."

In June 1951, two months after Buck's third birthday, he was delivered to Cotton Pershall. There was a tacit understanding in Nilo that Freehaven Muscles was Cotton's choice, and that King Buck was Olin's dog. Both men were right. Freehaven Muscles was a fine retriever—the sort that perpetuates fine bloodlines. But King Buck—the mid-sized Labrador of the fifty-dollar puppy price—was the sort that makes history. Under Cotton's hand the maturing King Buck began to catch fire.

In the spring of 1951, King Buck won a first, two seconds, and a third place. That fall he took another first, a third, and a fourth, and completed ten of eleven series of the 1951 National Championship Stake, placing high among the nation's top retrievers. He made a slow start in 1952 with a first and a third in the spring. In autumn he won a first, a second, and a fourth. In November he again entered the world series of retrievers at Weldon Spring, Missouri.

"King Buck seemed to have some power of knowing when the competition was really rough, and he always came through," Cotton said. "He wasn't a big dog as Labs go, but he had great style. Always quiet and well-behaved, not excitable or flashy. He just went steadily ahead with his job, series after series, whether on land or water."

Buck put on a show at Weldon Spring. He obeyed superbly, responded sharply to commands, and made direct, perfect retrieves. Right down to the final test, when he completed the tenth series with a 225-yard water retrieve, he performed like a champion.

Of a possible 300 points, King Buck had earned 294.9. The judges were vastly impressed with the new champion and vied with each other for superlatives: "Much style and hustle, lots of guts, very sharp, perfect response. The winner without question. "In all my experience, King Buck gave the best performance throughout the trial that I have ever seen . . ."

Soon after the trophy was awarded, Olin and his dog headed for Arkansas. Olin wished to see if Buck could perform as well in flooded timber as before a field trial gallery.

When Olin and his dog arrived in Stuttgart, the "Duck Hunting Capital of the World," the National Duck Calling Championship was just ending. Buck could not have had a more enthusiastic welcome; when he was introduced as the new national champion, he was given a booming ovation by the nation's finest waterfowlers.

Buck was the center of attention that night at a general rejoicing and was even offered some champagne in his silver trophy bowl. A champion athlete in training, he sensibly abstained. Olin poured out the champagne and filled the bowl with water, and after Buck had quenched his thirst, the bowl was refilled with champagne and passed among the guests as a communal toast to a great dog.

One man refused the toast. "I'm not going to drink from that bowl after a *dog* used it!!!" he exclaimed. At that time and place, the remark showed a signal lack of discretion. Under Olin's withering glare, the guest was invited to leave the festivities and seek more antiseptic surroundings. For a moment there was even a distinct possibility that he might find such a germ-free climate in the local emergency ward.

When Buck was taken to flooded timber for his first adventure with wild ducks and wild duck shooting, he came typically to life. Of King Buck, Olin said: "He was one of the finest wild duck retrievers I have ever seen. In spite of his intense field trial training, he loved natural hunting. He used his head in the wild, just as in field trials. That first wild duck shoot was *his* day, every minute of it, and he made the most of it. He was beautiful to watch."

Pershall continued to polish the champion that winter and spring, and although he was not entered in the spring trials, Buck swept the autumn campaigns with three first places. Then came his third National Championship Stake and the automatic defense of his new crown.

This contest was held at Easton, Maryland, in unseasonably warm weather—a long, tough competition that went into overtime. For the first nine series of the 1953 National the defending champion made perfect scores but was pressed closely. In the tenth series Buck needed special handling on a long marked triple, and the gap between his high scores and those of close competitors was narrowed. In the opinion of the judges, no dog

100

finishing the tenth series had a sufficient edge to be the winner. Two additional series were called. Buck went on to win with the flawless performance that John Olin and Dan Pomeroy watched from the chicken coop. By the twelfth series it was so apparent he was the clear winner that the official announcement came as an anticlimax.

Buck was active in the national field trial campaigns for four years after that, still competing fiercely with younger dogs and established champions. As late as 1957, when he was nine years old, he not only qualified for the National Championship Stake but also completed eleven series out of twelve in the National and nearly won another title!

During his years at Nilo, King Buck finished seventy-three of a possible seventy-five series in seven consecutive runnings of the National Championship Stake. The only series that he failed to complete in those seven Nationals were the eleventh series in the 1951 contest and the twelfth series in 1957.

There was still one major honor in store for the old champion. Maynard Reece, the famous Iowa artist whose work had already appeared on two duck stamps, came to Nilo and did a portrait of King Buck. The 1959 federal duck stamp was a portrait of old Buck with a drake mallard in his mouth, set against a backdrop of windswept marsh grass and flaring ducks. It was the first time a dog had ever appeared on a United States stamp.

King Buck died on March 28, 1962—just one week before his fourteenth birthday—and was placed in a small crypt at the kennel's entrance, his statue above him.

CHAPTER TWELVE

The Labrador Letter
By Joe Arnette

Dear Joe:

Remember me, Bill Jackson, from the years you worked in Idaho? It's been a good while—more than eight years—since we talked, so you may have to rewind your mental clock a bit to recall my name and who I am. Here's a memory jog that should help.

When you moved out of town, for a reassignment up north (to the backcountry, I believe it was), you gave me a two-year-old Labrador pup named Shade. As I remember, you could take only one dog with you and opted to keep your older Lab. You knew Shade would have a good home with me, but more than that—as you said—you knew how much I fancied him during the times we hunted together when he was a youngster.

But "fancied" became the wrong word after the first couple of months he was with me. The fact is that I loved the dog more with every year that passed. Outside of my wife and kids, he was the best thing that ever happened to me.

And now he is dead—I'll tell you about that in a minute—and I need your help to track down where he came from, where you got him, anything you know about his background. Not to replace him—he was unique in my mind—but to try to find another dog from a bloodline as close as possible to his. All I know is what is on his papers and what you told me when I took him: that Shade came from a deliberate breeding between a male and female owned by hunting partners of yours. Beyond that, I'm in the dark and have no clue how to contact these people.

First, the good part. I've had a fair number of Labradors over the past twenty years—decent dogs that were loyal, worked hard for me, and were good family members. You hunted behind one of them. They were all dogs that I cared about, but none of them approached Shade in any way.

You owned him during his beginning. You saw his potential and started developing it, but you couldn't foresee how deep that potential ran. (Thank goodness for that, or you wouldn't have given him to me.) You missed him when he began to blossom, then moved into the full flowering of his peak years. He was one of those dogs that looked promising—even good—as a youngster and became fine as an adult. At least from my view, Shade did everything to perfection.

I wish you could have seen him work the river. Think back to those sections that we hunted, where the current is powerful and the ducks tuck into the small backwaters and fingers. Remember, too, the straight runs where geese lift off the cornfields, then drop over the canyon rim to fly low along the water. I didn't keep a tally, but if Shade didn't pull two hundred birds a year from the river, I'll eat a raw goose—feet, feathers, and bill.

And pheasants? He flushed and fetched a bunch of birds for us as a pup, when you had him, but that was nothing compared to what he did—and how he did it—during the last eight years. He stayed steady, rarely lost a running bird, and never missed a mark no matter how long the retrieve. I even hunted him on valley quail along the river bluffs, ruffed grouse in the mountains, and sage grouse in the high desert. I've likely overworked this already, but Shade was a hell of a dog.

The dumbest thing I've ever done—or not done—was my failure to breed him. I never found a female that I thought was good enough. At least that's what I told myself. Though thinking back on it, and trying to be honest, I probably didn't look that hard; in truth, there are a lot of nice Labs in this part of the state. I suppose I was afraid that the pups wouldn't live up to Shade's standard. In that sense, I was avoiding any chance of disappointment rather than just accepting what turned out.

It could also be that Shade and I were so much a piece of each other's lives that I couldn't bring myself to share that relationship with another dog. Maybe that's it. And now I have nothing left from the best dog I'll ever own. Memories, yes, a mind full of them, but of Shade himself I have nothing.

And that brings me to the bad part. But first, I want to get something straight. Remember sitting in my workshop in those ratty chairs by the beer cooler, arguing about my letting my dogs run loose from time to time? Well, I heard what you were saying.

Understand that Shade never ran free unless I was with him. He was so devoted that I doubt he would have left home anyway, except to follow my truck, but it's important you understand that running loose had nothing to do with his death.

Whenever I was home, Shade lived inside with the rest of the family. During working hours, he stayed in a special kennel that I attached to the room off the workshop where I stored boats, boots, decoys, dog gear, and the like—you've been in it. I put a two-way door from the kennel into the room so he could get under cover when the weather turned rough. But, more often than not—and regardless of the weather—he preferred the room to the kennel. He never used the fancy, cedar-filled bed I put down for him. He made a nest on a pile of camo netting. I guess it smelled right.

Anyway, about two months ago, I got home from work and didn't see Shade in his kennel. At the sound of my truck pulling in, he'd always be sitting at the kennel door, tail thrashing, waiting to go wherever I was going. Then I called him. Nothing.

I found him in the storeroom, stretched over the camo pile with his head on one of my boots, which he'd yanked off the wall. He'd been dead several hours. From his appearance, it took a while for him to die. I still have nightmares about how bad, how twisted and stricken he looked lying in that room, surrounded by the things he loved.

I had my vet do a workup to find out what happened. Turns out it was one of the old coyote poisons that some ranchers still keep around and that a few still use, illegal or not. Shade also had two half-chewed, hard-boiled eggs in his stomach. Which means that someone drove up to my workshop, tossed the poisoned eggs into the kennel, perhaps watched the dog eat them, and then drove off.

Who or why? I have no idea and probably never will. But God help the sick son of a bitch if I find out. As far as I know, I don't have serious enemies—or at least none who would do something like that. Most people around here tend to be more direct. If they had a problem with me, it would be me they'd come after, not my dog. So, it seems, Shade was a target of pure meanness, the victim of an ugly act with no purpose other than to kill a dog. And that's the story of a wonderful partnership with a terrible ending.

I didn't intend to ramble on as I have, but in part I thought that you would want to know how Shade turned out and what ultimately happened to him. Mostly—though I know it's a long shot after all this time—I hope you can help me with some names and addresses of people who might have dogs from Shade's line. Thanks for staying with me through this letter.

I hope that you, your family, and your dogs are well.

Bill

CHAPTER THIRTEEN

Tales from the Dark Side
By Michael McIntosh

If memory serves me right, I have lived with dogs I could call my own for just about forty-three years now. With few exceptions, they have been gun dogs of one stripe or another; without exception, I have loved them all, loved them as fiercely and completely as they have loved me, shamelessly and without reserve. The roster of my dogs is fairly short—minuscule, by some standards—for I have always preferred to know them one at a time, two at the most, and nearly all have mercifully been long-lived and not prone to fatal accident.

By contrast, the list of dogs that have laid some claim on a place in my heart, however momentary the affair, is enormous, and would include almost every one I ever met. I have gone out of my way to make their acquaintance all over the world, gone out of pocket to see them fed and cared for when no one else was willing, gone half out of my head with grief at each loss of a dear old friend.

Simply put, I love dogs—large or little, yeoman or sissy,

working stiff or pampered pet. I have to confess, though, that I love gun dogs most of all. They like what I like, which is to poke around any shaggy piece of countryside where certain birds are likely to be found and to test our collective skills of nose and gun against their capabilities for survival and flight—exercises performed in the sheer animal exuberance of taking part, of being immersed in a world whose rhythms and mysteries are so vast that the deeper we penetrate, the more its margins fade away.

As my progress toward fifty years of being a hunter is about to come down to counting on a single hand, I can no longer tally all the dogs I've known. Some stand out sharp and clear. Others come to mind only in brief images. Many more shift and blend until I haven't a clue where one might end and another begins. I've known a few geniuses, a lot of competent craftsmen, and a handful of duds whose witlessness was mitigated only by their being lovable fools. I've known some men who deserved better dogs and some dogs that deserved better men. I've learned how easy it is to blame a dog for our own shortcomings, expecting too much and offering too little, how shamelessly we take credit that rightly belongs to them, how heart-crackingly and purely damn *good* it feels to see a piece of work pulled off with a flash of brilliance.

Fond as I am of dogs, I fancy it's not an unrealistic affection—though it certainly could be. We have a penchant for glorifying dogs beyond all the limits of reality and good sense, burdening them with fantastic presumptions of nobility and then growing disappointed and blameful when they can't possibly live up to it.

I can't think of a better way to illustrate just how far off the deep end we can go than simply to cite the lunkhead, whoever he was, who once observed that dog spelled backwards is *god*, as if it proved something. In response, I can only point out that buzzard spelled backwards is *drazzub*, polecat is *tacelop*, and the whole thesis strikes me as being so much *tihsesroh*. Dogs are not gods— unless, of course, we're willing to accept gods whose shortcomings sometimes are more than a match for their virtues. Dogs are simply dogs, which is enough to ensure that their concomitant disasters are more than sufficient. If I've learned anything in all these years, it's this: No creature that breathes is capable of delivering a wider range of realities more pointedly or more inescapably than a gun dog.

Now, I don't know if I've witnessed everything a gun dog can do that's either distressing, disgusting, disgraceful, disagreeable, distasteful, or some combination of two or more. Sometimes I hope so, because I'd hate to think it could get any worse.

I'm not talking about everyday lapses like tracking up the house with muddy feet, nor even such garden-variety misbehavior as selective deafness, breaking up other dogs' points, eating birds, or barreling out of a duck blind before called upon to do so. If those were the worst things dogs were capable of, then they truly would be candidates for the pantheon. The fact is, though, they are capable of much worse—acts of a magnitude to make saints fall a-cursing, behavior so vile and proclivities so foul as to gag a vulture at the very thought. Like the thorn beneath the rose, the dark side of the dog looms ever near the surface and manifests itself not so much when you least expect it but rather when it's least convenient, most embarrassing, or in some way certain to have maximum effect.

The fundamental themes that govern this shady realm are remarkably few. Perhaps this is because dogs are essentially simple creatures—and possibly because those who insist upon living with them are too. At any rate, these themes offer means as good as any for organizing a survey. In the interest of keeping this both accurate and in manageable proportion, the incidents I shall use by way of illustrating the points are strictly from my own experience or from reports by people I know to be reliable. Hard as it may be to believe, some men have been known to take liberties with the facts when relating dog stories, whether about their own dogs or others'. What you're about to read, though, is absolutely true, much as I wish most of it wasn't.

• • •

Strictly speaking, dogs are carnivores, just like their original ancestor, the wolf. Somewhere in the long evolutionary descent from *Canis lupus,* however, *Canis domesticus* acquired a gene, possibly several, that expanded its gustatory horizon considerably. The present-day dog is omnivorous in the broadest sense of the word, which is made up of two Latin words—*omnis,* or "all," and *vorare,* or "devouring." Together, they denote an organism willing to consume anything, and if you looked it up in an illustrated dictionary, you'd find a picture of a sporting dog.

Exactly which breed wouldn't really matter, although among the ones I've known, the most truly catholic tastes have belonged to Labrador retrievers. Sorting the big-leaguers from the amateurs isn't easy, but I'd have to give Burly a slight edge on all the rest. Burly was a big black Lab who belonged to an old friend of mine. He was a grand hunter and fearless retriever. He was also a first-rate companion—usually.

The thing about Burly was his appetite, both in quantity and variety. He was the only dog I ever knew who truly would eat *anything*. Which was fine so far as dog food and table scraps were concerned; we never had to go out of our way to keep him happy with what he was fed. The problem was all the stuff he'd find for himself; and even *that* would have been okay if his digestive system had been a match for his taste, or lack of same.

If I really put my mind to it, I probably could recall one or two trips that ended without Burly throwing up in the back of Jim's station wagon—but none occur to me off the top of my head. And it was never just some little wad of green grass, like every other dog hurls up now and then. No, when Burly unloaded, you just had to marvel that a mere eighty-five-pound dog could hold sixty pounds of dead fish, road-kill possum, deer guts, or whatever else he'd polished off while nobody was looking.

You could tell it wasn't going to be any dainty little burp just by listening. He'd suddenly stand up, pace back and forth a couple of times to find the exact geographical center of the cargo compartment, and then give forth a chorus of rumbling and churning that sounded like a volcano giving birth to New Zealand. This would culminate in the delivery of some wet, steaming, stinking mess that invariably arrived before Jim could get the car stopped alongside the road. Pulling over always gave old Burl the idea that we weren't through hunting yet, so he'd charge up to the front seat and give me one or two good slurps up the side of my face before I could fend him off. Nobody who ever went hunting with Burly had to ask twice why Jim carried an old shovel in the car.

On one occasion I wish I could forget, he even managed a double-header. Jim had moved to western Iowa by then, and I was up for a long weekend with pheasants. We let Burly out of his kennel the first morning, and he dashed around the house to air out. While Jim got the last of the gear loaded, I walked around to see if Burly was ready and met him coming the other way, just finishing breakfast, which in this case was a full-grown squirrel that he'd either caught fresh or found in the street out front.

Either way, it was impressive. I guess he didn't want to waste any hunting time, because he was in the process of swallowing the damn thing whole, and when I came along it was all down except one hind leg and the tail. Burl sort of humped up, took a couple of mighty heaves, and even those disappeared, tail and all. Not for long, though. It all came back up about twenty minutes later.

I don't know what it was he got hold of that afternoon; I'm not even sure a histologist could have made any sense of it, although he certainly would've had plenty to work with.

The last time I hunted with the old boy before he died, we parked the car next to a creek, which Burly naturally had to investigate while we uncased our guns. We could hear him still splashing around as we started off, so Jim whistled to get him moving. He came lumbering up the bank happily chewing on what I took to be a muskrat, judging from the tail.

"Burl's eating a muskrat," I called over to Jim.

Jim kept on walking. "That son of a bitch. There's probably a Number Four Victor trap on the other end of it." He sighed. "We'll find out on the way home."

• • •

One of the things in this life that I never asked for but got anyway is a strange knack for being nearby when two dogs decide to try tearing one another limb from limb. Rarely is one of the combatants mine, since I haven't had a male gun dog in more than twenty years, so I really don't understand why I'm always the one closest to the action. Just lucky, I guess.

I do know that I have little patience with dog fights and even less with the hammerheaded types that seem to make careers out of starting them. I am therefore apt to take draconian measures.

Water, I find, is a splendid tool for sorting out a donnybrook. I discovered this one day when two Labradors began disputing ownership of a dead duck in the bottom of a boat. (These fools had just spent four hours together in the same blind without raising an eyebrow or a hackle. Besides, the damn duck was *mine*, but try telling that to a dog.) They were in opposite ends of the boat, and I had one foot in and one in the water, when they met more or less between my legs and started snarling at one another. I grabbed the nearest collar, lost my balance, dragged the dog over the gunwale, and somehow managed to get him underneath me before I hit the water. I know it sounds amazing, but holding a

Labrador's head underwater for about five minutes makes him lose all interest in fighting.

On the whole, there's nothing funny about a dog fight until it's over, but I did see one that almost put me on my knees. It happened at a duck club in the Missouri River bottoms and involved two splendid young Labs and a newspaper sportswriter I used to hang out with in my teaching days.

Bill Bennett is a man who should never have owned even a picture of a dog. He loved them, but they were his nemesis. He was, for instance, the only man I've ever seen knocked flat on his face in a puddle of his own urine by a dog—but that's another story for another time. The fight I'm thinking of came after he bought the Labrador he named Ebony of Nghaerfyrddin, or some other equally inscrutable Welsh word that translated as "black dog with tail." Don't ask me why.

Even as a yearling pup, Ebby, as we called him, was magnificent, big and sleek and strong, and he showed all the promise of becoming a first-rate hunter. The day we shot at Greenhead Farm, we showed up about ten minutes late and found a local physician in our blind. While he very graciously apologized for having misread the blind assignments on the clubhouse wall, his dog, who was somewhat older than Ebby and grouchy as a Cape buffalo with a case of jock itch, growled and snarled. I was not unhappy to see him led away across a field of cut corn.

We gave neither of them a thought until the end of the day, when the good doctor winged a mallard that sailed way out into the corn before going down. Since we had a better view of where it fell than he did, I suggested we go help him retrieve it. Bill put Ebby on a leash, and we waded across our pool and into corn stubble almost knee-deep with the slick, gluey northwest-Missouri mud that is a major factor in what holds the world together. Miserable stuff to walk in.

Doc and his dog were out of their blind, too, headed down the field, and when the Lab saw us coming, he wheeled around and charged straight for us. He wasn't making very speedy headway, but we couldn't, either, so I told Bill to get a good grip on the leash and I'd try to stop this maniac before he reached Ebby.

It almost worked. I got my fingertips on his collar, but he ducked his head and I lost him. In the next instant, he bowled into Bill and Ebby, and all three went down in one massive tangle of arms, legs, dogs, flying mud, snarling, snapping, and half-coherent shouting.

Even if he hadn't had the leash wrapped around his wrist, Bill was as helpless against the mud as a turtle on its back. The whole pile kept rolling over and over, although somehow Bill managed to stay mostly on the bottom. For all the uproar, the dogs were scarcely touching one another, but between them they were literally stomping poor Bill into the mud. Everything he tried to say ended up choked off in midphrase—which was just as well, because none of it was fit for tender ears anyway.

It was a great show, and I enjoyed it as much as I dared, but finally it was clear that either I had to do something right then, or drag Bennett's carcass out of the field later. Big as the dogs were, they were flyweights compared with him, so I waded over and grabbed the first collar that came to the top of the heap. Mercifully, the other dog was wearing it. By the time I got the collar twisted into a passable form of tourniquet and managed to turn Old Crusher's attention from trying to fight to trying to breathe, Doc came slogging up, red-faced with exertion, eyes the size of teacups. I handed over his dog, and the last we saw of them, they were headed back for the clubhouse, Doc delivering a very loud lecture on aspects of Labrador parentage that I'm sure aren't listed anywhere in the Field Dog Stud Book.

On the way home, Bill rehearsed a similar dissertation that may have included some observations on my own ancestry, but I'm really not sure. It's hard to understand a man who's trying to talk and spit at the same time. Besides, all I did was suggest that if he ever got tired of journalism, he could have a great career in mud wrestling.

CHAPTER FOURTEEN

The Marsh
By Jim Spencer

Pintails generally don't decoy very well, but these two had evidently forgotten to read the book. They made one high, down-wind pass, spotted the decoy spread in the lee of the stand of roseaux cane, and heeled over like thirsty cropdusters at quitting time. They came beating their way back into the stiff wind, wings laboring, losing altitude in preparation for landing with their newfound friends.

John, the man, and Lum, the dog, let them come. The two old hunting partners crouched side by side in a modified Cajun pirogue, which was jammed by its oars against the nearly solid wall of roseaux and hidden by a makeshift blind of freshly cut cane stalks stuck up in the mud in front of the boat.

The big Labrador whined softly, shivering with eagerness as he watched the two gray ducks coming slowly on. John smiled, cutting his eyes at Lum for a second, then whispered, "Quiet." The black dog glanced guiltily at John before returning his attention to the brace of bull pintails, which were now hovering inside the outer edge of the decoys, reaching for the water with their feet.

John was sitting in one end of the little boat with a wear-silvered Model 12 across his knees. He swung the stock to his shoulder and pushed the barrel through an opening in the cane blind. John wasn't consciously aware of pulling the trigger, but he knew he had done so because the nearest pintail seemed to fly into an invisible barrier. Its outline blurred and it dropped among the bobbing decoys.

The remaining duck opened up and caught wingfuls of wind, putting yardage between himself and danger, but he never really had a chance. The spent hull was still in the air when John's gun roared again, and the pattern neatly centered the departing sprig. The strong wind carried the duck in a long arc and he fell more than eighty yards from the blind, sending up a great geyser of water.

"Get 'em, Lum!" John said unnecessarily. The big dog had already launched himself, nearly upsetting the pirogue on takeoff. Lum hit the brackish, muddy water and went completely under, bursting back to the surface at once. Snorting loudly, he struck off down the wind, ignoring the nearest duck for the moment. John settled back to watch the performance.

It took Lum only thirty seconds to reach the distant pintail, but the return trip against the wind was more time-consuming. Waves were running high across the mud flat, and the big duck created additional drag. But Lum finally made it, paws churning madly, and deposited the soggy duck over the gunwale of the pirogue, then swam for the other bird.

Moments later, both ducks and the dog were in the boat after some fancy teeter-tottering by John during the boarding process. Lum grinned and gave John the customary shower of muddy water, and although John turned his back and shielded himself as well as he could, in the close quarters of the Cajun boat there was no place to hide.

"One of these days I'm going to get you your own boat," John told the dog. He reached out and roughed the Lab's damp ear. Lum grinned again and snapped playfully at the offending hand.

"Oh, no you don't," John said. "This boat ain't big enough for roughhousing. Anyway, we're on a duck hunt, so get your head down. We got some takers."

The flock of gadwalls came in low with no preliminaries, and when John came up to shoot they flared. His swing was hampered by the canes he had stuck in front of the blind to hide it, and the whole bunch of ducks was out of range before he untangled the gun barrel. Lum gave him a quizzical look and whined softly.

"Shut up," John answered grumpily. "Cane got in my way. What do you care, anyway? This way you don't have to get wet."

Another bunch of ducks, mostly gadwalls, decoyed beautifully a few minutes later, and the cane got in the way again as the ducks flared to the side instead of straight up. Lum sighed audibly, whirligigged slowly in a tight circle, and flopped down with a grunt, his back to John.

"Well, I'll be . . ." John said. "Hey, Lum! Are you quitting me?" He grinned at the black dog curled up in the bottom of the pirogue. The dog ignored him.

The sky was getting darker, John thought as he scanned the air for more ducks. The wind was really howling in off the Gulf now, bending the tops of the roseaux cane out over the pirogue.

"That should be plenty of cover without all this timber up here blocking my swing," John said. He laid the Model 12 down and jerked up the dozen or so stalks of cane and stuffed them into the growth behind the boat.

The sky was full of ducks upset by the approaching weather. They were everywhere, so John called only sparingly, letting the decoys do most of the work. Now that he had a clear field of fire, he kept the Labrador busy. There were enough ducks working so that he could afford to pick and choose, and when the tenth duck fell there was only one gadwall in the bunch. All the rest were bull pintails, very fine ducks that carried only a ten-point value this year.

Lum made a long, laboring retrieve of the final bird while John struggled around in the muck and waist-deep brackish water, pulling up the decoys and wrapping the strings around their necks, nearly bogging down a half dozen times in the process. After he helped the tired old Lab into the pirogue, John pulled his head in like a turtle as Lum gave him the traditional shower. Clambering aboard at the other end of the boat, John freed it from the stand of cane and began the long pull across the open marsh to the tarpaper shack, which served as the hunting camp some two miles away across the windswept open marsh. He poled easily, with an economy of motion learned over five decades of repetition.

Afterward, John could never say just how it happened. One second he stood confidently in the stern of the pirogue, knees rolling with the waves as he shoved the little boat crosswind toward the camp that was barely visible across the choppy expanse of salt flat. Lum was perched in the bow as was his habit, barking puppyishly at the flocks of ducks, gulls, snipe, and willets wheeling in the gray sky above. The next second found both man and dog coughing and snorting as they struggled to keep their heads above the two-foot waves. The overturned pirogue bobbed in the water near them.

John tried to reach the upended boat, but the heavy waders he was wearing made it impossible to buck the rough water. During the thirty seconds it took him to struggle out of the boots, the pirogue either sank or was lost from view in the rough water.

A surge of panic hit him and he began striking blindly at the water, the way a man fights a swarm of bees. Almost immediately one of his flailing fists hit something rough and hairy, and John opened his eyes to look into the face of the big Labrador. The sight of the dog treading water beside him steadied John's nerves, and his panic left as quickly as it had arrived. Trying to think as rationally as he could, he assessed their predicament. At best, the outlook was grim.

First, the pirogue had overturned in the middle of a large peat burn—a natural pond made by fires that burn away the organic soil, leaving deep holes in the otherwise shallow marsh. And, as John knew too well, they were several hundred yards from wadeable water.

Second, the temperature was cold for southern Louisiana, hovering right at the freezing mark. Coupled with the stiff wind that was blowing, the chill factor was nearly zero. Dying of exposure was a definite threat even if they did make it to shallow water.

Third, the mishap had occurred well over a mile across open marsh from the camp, and John was doubtful of his ability to wallow through the clinging mud for that distance.

All this flashed through his mind in the space of a heartbeat, and for the space of another heartbeat John almost decided to give up. But an anxious whine from the Lab brought him back to the reality of the situation. He couldn't give up, not when the big dog, with all his instincts telling him to strike out downwind, still held back and stayed close to his master. As scared as he was, John felt a rush of love for the Labrador treading water beside him.

"Well, old fella," he shouted above the thirty-knot wind, "let's give it a try!" They set off downwind, staying close together and swimming slowly, trying to conserve as much of their energy as they could.

The swim proved tough going for John. His heavy clothes were waterlogged—they hampered his movements and dragged him down so the whitecapping waves broke over his head. He quickly discovered how to time his breathing to keep from choking, though by the time they had covered half the distance to shallow water, John was disoriented and half-strangled from being tossed and rolled repeatedly beneath the water's surface by the now three-foot waves.

But Lum stayed as close to the old man as he could, wanting

to help but not knowing how. Occasionally he would nudge John's shoulder or face with his nose. It was this contact as much as John's own strong will that kept him afloat long enough to reach the edge of the peat burn.

John was almost gone when his feet struck mud. The footing was too soft to support him at first, but as the water shallowed, the mud firmed, and before long he found it would partially support the weight of his submerged body. As soon as he was able, John stopped swimming and stood still in the deep muck, coughing, gasping for breath, and shivering uncontrollably. The dog whined uneasily, still treading water, plainly expressing his desire to keep moving toward the pass bank where they would be able to find solid ground.

The cold was a living thing, eating its way into John's mind and body, numbing his brain as well as his muscles. He had been in the water for more than five minutes now, and he felt drowsy. He smiled faintly as he thought of how good a nap would feel right now.

Lum barked loudly and John snapped his eyes open without ever knowing they had been closed, his smile giving way to a grimace. "Okay, okay!" he shouted fiercely, angry at himself for his weakness and feeling that very anger sending warmth to his numbed limbs. "I hear you! I'm coming!" He set off thrashing across the marsh, fighting mud covered by water which was still forming waves that broke over his head with a maddening regularity. He was nearly blinded and half-choked by the brackish water, but for the first time since the pirogue had tossed him out,

John felt that he was going to make it. He struggled quietly beside the dog, concentrating on each step with fierce intensity.

The water was shallower now. Only a few inches covered the mud, and the waves, which were mostly mud themselves, were running less than a foot high. But the mud itself was worse here, and John's rate of progress was slower as the sucking ooze tried to pull him back.

Beside him, the grizzled Labrador was also tiring. Lum was still more or less swimming through the soupy mud, his tongue dragging in it and his breath coming in short, irregular gasps as he struggled forward. John watched him and thought, "My God, what if the old devil has a heart attack?" He stopped abruptly, leaned back and more or less sat in the mud, half-reclining and half-floating.

"Here, boy!" he called, clapping his numb hands together and wincing at the pain that resulted. "Come on, Lum! Let's rest for a little while."

The black dog's muddy head swung around and Lum, nearly spent, looked dully at his master. His matted, mud-clubbed tail made a feeble attempt at a wag. He whined and pushed on toward the pass bank, and John had to call again, "Here, Lum! Come back here, fella!"

The dog slowed, stopped, looked around again, and cocked his head. He pushed on for another ten feet, stopped again and barked loudly. Plainly, the Labrador didn't want to stop. This one-voiced argument went on for the space of perhaps three minutes, and finally, John bowed to superior instinct.

"Okay," John shouted over the gusting wind. "Maybe you're right. But at least I got a little rest while we were arguing. I can make it now."

With that he started forward again. Or attempted to. The stop had been a bad move. While he remained in one spot, his body had sunk deeper into the muck. To his horror, John found he was unable to move.

The panic he had felt when the pirogue first swamped came washing back over him like a fog. He began struggling wildly, but this only served to sink his body deeper into the mud. Drawing on his inner reserves, John forced himself to be calm,and he stopped fighting the mud. He called to the dog again, who was waiting ten yards ahead for him to catch up. It took all of his self-control to keep from screaming.

"Lum!" he shouted in an almost calm voice. "Go to the camp, boy! Go get Bill!"

The dog pricked up his ears and whined, knowing he was being given an order but failing to grasp the idea. He came back toward John a few yards and stopped, looking intently into his master's face and searching his eyes for some clue.

"Bill!" John repeated, struggling to keep the hysteria out of his voice and wracking his brain for a way to make the dog under-stand. "Go get Bill. Fetch, Lum! Go get 'em, boy!"

The dog's expression registered puzzlement as he listened to the jumble of words. Cocking his head in the familiar pose, he listened as John repeated the same phrases time after time.

When understanding came it was with the suddenness of an

electrical switch being thrown. Lum snapped his head upright, barked loudly one time, and began churning through the mud and water in the direction of the tantalizingly close pass bank.

The bottom grew firmer as Lum neared the natural levee flanking Pass-a-Loutre. His lunges gradually changed into yardage-eating leaps, and the leaps turned into a sliding run across the mud flat as he reached first the edge of the water, then the truly firm, high ground of the pass bank. He stopped for a moment to look out across the two hundred yards of mud flat separating him from his master.

Out in the marsh, John was watching as the dog turned to look. He waved an arm in the *Look over there* signal he used when directing Lum to a fallen duck. He could barely hear the dog's answering bark above the increasing wind.

And then he was gone, disappearing into the thick brush without a trace, running silently and swiftly toward the mile-distant hunting shack in search of Bill, John's forty-year-old son who, along with his own teenage son, Johnny, was sharing the camp with the old man this weekend.

"Well, if that ain't something," John said half-aloud after the muddy, black shape had disappeared like a wraith. "Just like Rin Tin Tin."

John steeled himself for the wait, flexing what muscles he could without making himself sink deeper into the mire. The deadly chill was creeping back into his bones since he had stopped moving, and he tried to keep his mind busy to ward off the drowsiness he knew was coming. He started talking aloud, thinking that the sound of his own voice might help keep him awake.

"He sure was an unlikely looking puppy when Bill gave him to me!" the old man yelled at a passing marsh hawk, causing the bird to veer away downwind. "Runty-looking little fellow, he was. He sure fooled me. Fooled a lot of other people, too. I still think Bill gave him to me as a joke, at first. But it backfired. Best dog in Louisiana."

John's voice lowered as his thoughts turned inward, then faded away altogether as he grew colder and colder, his resistance to the deadly drowsiness slipping with each passing minute. But his thoughts went on, wandering aimlessly through the past.

Funny, the old man thought, some of the little things you remember. Like the sight of the puppy and the grandson asleep together in the doghouse. Or the time little Johnny came back to the house mad because—because Lum went fishing with him and—kept—swimming out after the—cork—and—bringing it back in—it sure was getting sleepy out here!—wish there were gonna—be—some more mem'ries—too bad—too bad a fella— fella—makes fool outta m'self when gets old—not my fault, though—silly little boats—ain't first man do that out here—also ain't first man die 'count of it out here—

"—*didn't think we'd find him.*" The words, and the sound of his son's voice, penetrated the fog in John's head, and he slowly came back to consciousness. He opened one eye and immediately the worried faces of his son and grandson appeared above him.

The old man looked around at the porthole beside him and

surveyed the small cabin in which he found himself. A feeling of motion and the muted growl of a diesel engine told him he was aboard a powerful, rapidly moving boat.

"What . . . ?" he started to ask, but his son cut him off.

"Be quiet, Pop," Bill said. "You're going to be okay. We're on a Wildlife and Fisheries Commission boat, and we're on the way to Venice. Before you know it you'll be in a hospital bed."

The words came pouring out of his son in a flood of relief, and the old man smiled in spite of the pain in his cold, tortured muscles when he was told how Lum had brought Bill and Johnny in true wonder-dog fashion to the mud flat where John lay unconscious and near-dead in the clinging mud.

The Commission boat had been on its regular patrol of the area, stopping at each of the sixteen hunting shacks on the game-management area. The boat came chugging down the pass as Bill and Johnny dragged the old man to dry ground, and in minutes they were aboard and flying upriver to Venice. It was a—

John finally interrupted his son's exciting monologue and demanded weakly, "Where's my Lum-dog?"

At the sound of his name the anxious Labrador bolted up from the floor and stuck his head and still-muddy forequarters into the cramped berth where the old man lay. Heedless of the mud, John wrapped both arms around Lum's great head and buried his face in the grimy coat, holding tightly while the dog licked his ear.

When John released Lum it was hard to tell which of the two was more muddy. The dog wormed his way up into the bunk space with the old man, who moved over to make more room. Bill opened his mouth as if to order the dog down, but John raised a hand to silence him.

"This old soldier has more right to be in this bunk than I do, son," John said quietly. "He's the one who did all the work today." He laid a loving hand on Lum's muddy flank and received a tired but contented grunt in response. In a matter of seconds, the two old hunting partners were sleeping peacefully.

CHAPTER FIFTEEN

One
by Gene Hill

I admired the dog out of courtesy and that was about it. He wasn't anything special to look at—just your nice, solid, big-headed black Lab. I've seen hundreds just like him, give or take an inch here or a detail there. His work in the field was efficient, but not exciting. He wasn't what a real trial man would call steady, and as often as not he'd drop a goose to readjust a hold, generally preferring to drag it along by a wing. He did have one peculiar habit I noticed—he never picked up a bird, no matter how dead it was, without first stepping on the neck with one foot and hold-ing it there until he'd grabbed the wing. I asked about this, and his owner told me it was a habit he'd had since his first goose pecked him pretty bad. This bit of cause-and-effect reasoning pleased me, being a "once burned, twice shy" person myself.

This day in a goose pit on the eastern shore of Maryland was as common as the surrounding mud. Intermittent flights had us calling, more for the amusement of it than for any real hope of turning them. But every so often, a pair or a small flock of five or six would toll close enough for a shot, and since we were in no hurry or that anxious to take geese, we took turns gunning. By mid-afternoon we each had two geese, enough for our personal satisfaction; but the weather was mild, so we had come to a mutual unspoken agreement to just sit there and chat rather than pick up and go our separate ways. It was a lovely way to spend an afternoon: gunning talk mostly, a little fishing talk, some book titles exchanged—just your average small talk between two strangers. We found common ground and an occasional bit of laughter that sweetened the conversation, putting each of us at ease, wanting the other to find us good company . . . a small, pleasant, spontaneous friendship.

He hardly mentioned his Lab, and neither did I, but I was pleased to notice that the dog sat leaning a little against his master's leg or put his head on the man's foot when he chose to lie do, and that my companion's hand was stroking the dog or messing with his ears or scratching him behind the neck. It was just the sort of thing any one of us might do, an ordinary circumstance, a commonplace relationship. Nor did I find it strange that the dog paid absolutely no attention to me whatsoever. There are dogs that are nuisances for affection (several of mine were like that, from being spoiled and encouraged to play), and others that prefer to keep to themselves, and still others that are clearly one-person creatures.

He had not bothered to bring a lunch, but I, for once, had gotten myself together and packed one. When I do get the lunch-making urge, I tend to go overboard and had more than enough to share, which I gladly did. We each had two sandwiches, and as he ate his, he fed the other to his dog at the same pace, bite for bite. A sandwich and a half was enough for me, so I offered the dog the half left over. He wouldn't touch it from my hand, so I placed it on the floor of the blind in front of him where it sat unnoticed and untasted until I asked my friend if the dog were on some sort of self-imposed diet.

"No, I don't think so," he laughed. He picked up the food and as before, fed it to the dog bite by bite.

You can usually sense when someone has been waiting for a chance to talk about something that needs to be aired. You feel that he's been looking for the right time and place and ear. I was hoping that I'd have that privilege, so I just sat there and watched him dribble pieces of that sandwich, pieces about the size of 00 Buck, to a dog that was not only used to this little game, but so delighted with it that he was making soft moaning noises and rolling his eyes like a fundamentalist convert.

"Pete, here is about the worst dog I've ever owned," he said with some hesitation, "but he's taught me more about dogs, in a strange way, than most of the others I've had—and there have been quite a few."

I just sat there and stared at the floor of the blind, not wanting to look at him, because he didn't want to look at me. Right now he wanted a listener, a sympathetic and understanding one; one who had some knowledge of what he was talking about. But not a conversation—just an ear would do fine for the time being.

"If you've ever followed the field trial circuit, you probably know my name. For quite a few years I was the amateur trainer

135

that most of the pros worried about. And they had good reason. I had the money, the time, the drive, and the dogs. And you needed all that just to start because you were in against the Belmonts, the Roosevelts, big steel money, big oil money, and just plain *money*—so big that hardly anyone remembered where it had all come from. One handler drove his dogs to the trials in an old Rolls Royce fitted up like a kennel truck; the people he worked for drove Rolls', and they didn't want their dogs in anything less! I didn't go that far . . . but I wasn't too far behind. I've chartered more than one plane to take my dogs where I thought they ought to be running, and I never regretted a penny of it.

"I even had Purdey make me a pair of side-bys just for field-trial gunning in case my dogs didn't finish, so I'd still be part of the action. You learn a lot about certain dogs when you're a gun, but that's getting a little away from my story.

"It all started simply enough, and typically as far as I'm concerned. I've always loved competition; I've been a top-flight amateur golfer, a tournament winner on the trap and skeet circuit, and got to where they knew I was there in the live-bird rings of Madrid and Monte Carlo. Then I got to thinking about getting a dog.

I traveled so much in my early days that owning one didn't make much sense. When I went shooting, my hosts all had fine kennels, so it didn't make much difference if I had my own dog or not. In fact, it was better that I didn't. But when a big holding company bought me out for more money than I could ever spend and moved me up to some spot that was all title and no work, I began to look around for something new to take up. It was just about destined that I would start field-trialing Labs.

"I'd been a member of one of those fancy Long Island duck clubs for years and had seen some pretty good dogs. It might sound silly, but I believe that a man has to have a dog, and a breed of dog, that suits his personality. If I believed in reincarnation I don't doubt that I'd come back as a Lab—or would like to. It's a little vain, I know, but I saw myself as brave, honest, and strong, as Hemingway might have put it, and that's what I like about the Lab. It's all up front, nothing held back.

"Anyway, one of my duck hunting buddies at the old Sprig Club had a litter of dogs out of good field-trial stock and he gave me a male as sort of a retirement present. He said that at worst, he'd be somebody I could talk to and take care of and get the same in return. After I'd spent a few weeks with the pup, I decided to have a professional take a look at him. I felt he might have what it would take to be a trial dog, but I believe in the opinions of the people who do it everyday, not just an amateur appraisal.

"The professional not only liked the dog but made an offer then and there to take him for training, and I agreed. He had a fine reputation and I liked his whole approach to the training idea. He was to start the dog, and when he was satisfied, I'd come down and spend a week or so with him and learn to run the dog myself. Then I'd get a training schedule to work on and would check back with him for a few days on a regular basis. If the dog did exceptionally well, he'd take him over completely and campaign in the major stakes.

"His name was Wonderdog—because I wondered what I'd do

with him when I first got him; a little joke with myself. If you follow the retrievers, you know how far he got and what a piece of pure bad luck it was that he didn't become National Champion. He was killed a little while after his first Nationals when an assistant trainer was in an accident, and the dog trailer was totally demolished. I was hurt by the loss, of course, but by then I was committed to try for another dog as good as he was. He'd sired a litter and I arranged to get the pick for stud service.

"If anything, the pup was better than his father; a bit more aggressive and strangely, a bit more biddable. It was almost as if he felt destined to compete and understood what was expected of him all along. I called him Little Wonder—another private joke with myself. Almost everyone was soon calling him One, short for number one because that's what he looked like right from the start. He was one of the hottest derby dogs anyone had seen when he was right, and he usually was. I'd never thought of a dog as an athlete before One, but when he took to water he reminded me of a diver—I know it's silly to think of a dog having 'form,' but he did—and I never got over the idea that he knew it and worked at it.

"By the time he was three, One had totally captivated the trial circuit—not just in wins and placements, but by his personality, his pure competitiveness, and his genius for doing just the right thing at the right time. I know for sure that more than one judge laid out a series with just him in mind, but as hard as they tried to challenge him, he was usually up to it. Of course, he had an off-day now and then, disinterested or bored or maybe tired, but even then he did his job—just without the fire he was famous for. In his first National at Bombay Hook he placed third. I don't think he deserved to win, but he did deserve second. The head judge and I weren't exactly friends, since I'd beaten his dog at several important trials and he wasn't above playing a little politics with some nationally known names.

"I'd planned to retire One after his first in the Nationals, and just use him as a stud dog and gunning companion. We'd become pretty close and I thought he deserved a little rest and some fun—some of the fun had gone out of the competition as far as I was concerned. But I did want that win for him in the worst way. He'd worked hard for it and most of us still believed that he had the class and the talent to go all the way. If any dog deserved it, One certainly did. The more we worked him that season, the sharper he got. I didn't think there was much room for improvement, but in subtle ways, he just looked better. His long blinds were precision itself, and when he was stopped to the whistle, he really stopped. It was as if he were reading your mind. I heard one judge remark in a friendly way that he looked as if he were showing off. I'm making him sound as if he were absolutely perfect, but he did have one small fault. Every now and then, for some reason, he'd make one or two little yelps on a retrieve on land. I always put it down as pure enthusiasm, and the trainer and I had long given up trying to make him stop. More often than not, we'd be the only ones to notice it."

Here he paused for so long I didn't think he was going to go on with the rest of the story. He was rumpling his dog and searching for the right words and the strength to say them. I had the feeling this was a story that he'd never told before and perhaps didn't want to tell now—yet knew that he must so he could get a different grip on it himself. For some strange reason I thought of the words to an old song about "hanging your tears out to dry." How perfectly put; how perfectly true.

For the first time since he'd begun, he turned to look at me and I could see the gray, sad sparkle of small tears. I turned away a bit to give him a moment of privacy. He covered his face with his handkerchief for just a second and went on.

"I'd say the chances of what happened ever happening are more than one in a million. One of those random tragedies that always seem to strike the innocent; the casual passerby. There was a strand of wire, just one, that was only about two feet long between an old post and a tree. I'd heard One making his odd yipping noise and suddenly he went end-over-end in the air and lay still. Both the judges and I rushed out knowing instantly that something fearful had happened, and there was One, stretched out, dead from a broken neck. A small trickle of blood ran down the corners of his jaw where he'd run into the wire with his mouth open.

"I carried him back to the station wagon and put him on the front seat and started to drive. I don't remember how long it was or where I went, but I do remember that I kept rubbing his head, believing for the longest time that he'd suddenly sit up and everything would be all right. Today is the second time in my life that I've cried; that was the first.

"There's a small graveyard behind the lodge at the Sprig Club where our special dogs were put to rest, and the whole club turned out to help me put him there. I had a blanket made of his ribbons and my gunning coat was his pillow. He always loved to sleep on that whenever he had the chance. One of the members read a list of his wins and when finished with that, he paused, and in a soft tenor began to sing 'Auld Lang Syne,' and everyone, except me, joined in with him."

He stopped again for a minute and blew his nose; I must confess I did the same.

"I virtually stopped gunning for a long time after that. When people asked me why, I told them that my favorite partner had passed away. Almost none of them ever thought that it might have been just my dog. Funny, isn't it, how not many understand the relationship a man can have with his dog? And yet, I can tell you now that there are few, if any, things in my life that meant as much to me as One, and how odd but true that an emptiness like that is there forever.

"It's been about five years since I lost One, and last fall, a friend of mine, the same one that sang that afternoon at the duck club, came to my house and rang the bell. When I opened the door he reached in and put a puppy in my arms, saying, 'It's about time Pete had someone to look after,' and then he turned and left.

"This is Pete." At the sound of his name, Pete looked up and made some sort of a face that I'll say was as close to smiling as a dog can get.

"When I said that Pete was the worst of my dogs, I didn't

141

mean anything except that I never trained him. I just let him be Pete. And that's been enough, more than enough. They say that a man deserves one good dog in his life . . . but that's not true. I've had a couple, and in his own way, Pete's right there in my heart with them all now. It's a full space with two empty ones beside it, if you can see it that way."

I nodded to let him know that I agreed, but I didn't say anything, because I didn't think anything needed to be said at just that moment.

He began, after a little while, to talk about something else, and after giving me his card, he thanked me for listening and said it was time for him and Pete to be heading on home. I said goodbye and told him that I'd wait here a little while longer in the blind just to watch the sun come down. But that wasn't the whole truth. What I wanted to do was sit there in the quiet of twilight and hear the soft phrases of that ancient Scottish melody again in my mind, and picture the scene of that group of men singing a dog into eternity, comforting themselves in the timeless ritual of shared sorrow and the understanding of loss.

In the last light, I slung my two geese over my shoulder and started back to where I'd left the car. I found myself softly singing what I could remember of One's funeral song, and suprisingly, I wasn't as saddened by the idea as you'd imagine. The saving thought was one of remembrance; as long as a man lives, so will his dogs in one form or another . . . in a story or a song. One will always be there to take care of the other, and I can't think of a nicer way to put it than we will *share a cup of kindness now . . .*

CHAPTER SIXTEEN

Just Me and Daisey
By Pete McLain

It's Christmas Eve, the wind is blowing forty miles an hour, the thermometer reads fifteen degrees, and you want to go duck shooting?

That was the answer I got from several friends when I asked them to join me for a duck hunt on New Jersey's Barnegat Bay last December 24th. During the early season I would have had a dozen takers, but not today. I was tempted to scuttle the idea myself—weather conditions were almost impossible for both man and ducks—but experience has taught me one thing: When it's not fit to go duck shooting, that's the time to go!

When I walked out of the back door in insulated waders and an old camouflage parka, carrying the well-worn Browning autoloader, Daisey—my eight-year-old Labrador retriever—almost climbed the kennel fence with excitement. I thought to myself that she ought to be in the warm doghouse hiding, but good Labs aren't built that way.

When we arrived at the boat dock near Barnegat Inlet, the bone-chilling northwest wind was gusting at forty-five miles per hour. The tops of the four-foot waves froze and looked like smoke hanging over the churning bay. I headed the bow of the small skiff into the wind, and the seas began to smash against the hull, sending sheets of salt water over our heads and coating the inside of the boat with a layer of ice.

"What the hell are we doing here today?" I asked Daisey, who looked back at me like I was as crazy as I suspected I was. But I was starved for a day of old-fashioned duck shooting, and this looked like just the day for it.

As we beat our way up the narrow channel toward my gunning shack on a small island in Barnegat Bay, I prayed that the outboard engine would not act up, or that the boat would not take on so much ice that we would lose speed and power. Winter on the water is unforgiving and even a minor mistake can be deadly. Just two weeks before, two duck hunters had drowned about a mile away from us when a decoy line tangled in their propeller, stalling the engine and causing the boat to swamp and sink.

At the houseboat, I warmed myself in front of the gas oven, lit the wood-burning stove, and gathered up eight of my best cork decoys. After loading a gunning coffin with decoys, shells, and extra clothing, I towed the coffin with a Barnegat Bay sneakbox and a four-horsepower engine about half a mile to a small cove where the black ducks and mallards had been feeding heavily on the millions of killie fish that were concentrating to hibernate in the mud. This doesn't make the ducks taste any better, but it quickly puts on several ounces of body fat that they need to endure winter weather like today's.

The wind chill factor was well below zero, and ice was freezing all over Daisey and the sneakbox's spray curtain. I buried my face in the corner of my down parka's hood and peeked out occasionally to see where we were going. Daisey could have hunkered down in the dog compartment of my sneakbox, but she sat up, facing the weather and watching the hundreds of ducks that were flooding from the open bay, seeking the protection of the marsh. There were ducks everywhere we looked. A cloud of brant circled around looking for protected water, but there was none due to the high tide and strong wind. The weatherman called for an arctic front to bring near-zero temperatures and snow for Christmas. The waterfowl knew the forecast better than the U.S. Weather Service.

"Here we are," I told Daisey, "three hours of work to get to this little cover. I hope it's worth the effort." Like many hunters, when I'm alone with gun dogs, I frequently talk to them—and I suspect they understand. But when I hunt with partners, I seldom speak directly to dogs other than to praise or admonish them.

I set the decoys within thirty feet of the bank and positioned the gunning coffin so I could swing easily to the right, being a left-handed shooter. The marsh grass was only a couple of inches high and there was no other cover to hide the coffin, so I covered it with frozen eelgrass that had been windrowed around the cove. It wasn't the best of hides, but I thought it would work in this weather. I moved the sneakbox a few hundred yards upwind to hide it from the ducks on their approach to the decoys.

Hunting from the short grass of a tidal marsh is a real trick.

Because you have to lie on your back inside the coffin, you can't watch the birds approach. You can't sit up and look around, and when shooting from a sitting position your gun-swing angle is less than forty-five degrees. When a duck crosses the bill of your cap, you come up shooting.

Hiding a dog under these conditions can also be a problem. Usually, I carry special fiberglass dog boxes that are watertight and provide a retriever with protection from the wind. However, today we had to travel light and fast, and there was no room for Daisey's box. I made a nest for her out of eelgrass on the lee side of the coffin to provide at least a small break from the icy wind. I have hunted with retrievers all my life, but I still marvel at how these dogs can swim in the ice cold water, shake off, and then sit in near-zero temperatures—and love it.

Before I was down in the coffin and loaded, two big, red-legged black ducks were hanging over the decoys, straining their necks like they were on a string. I remembered that this year, black ducks had a point value of one hundred, which amounted to a one-bird bag limit. To go through all this for a single bird would have been foolish, so I decided to shoot only male mallards with a value of twenty-five points each. This would allow for a four-bird limit. From where I was lying, looking into the north-east wind, all the black ducks in the Atlantic Flyway appeared to be coming my way. A couple thousand blacks and mallards were flying in every direction.

I let a dozen blacks flirt with my decoys as I waited for a drake mallard. One suddenly came from behind me and skidded over the decoys. He made a quick climb, a tight turn, and just at the peak of the turn, I pulled on him. It was one of those shots where you kill the bird stone-dead in the air and it simply stops flying and falls into the decoys.

"Back!" I yelled at Daisey. She hit the water with a great splash, swam through the decoys, and returned with my first duck. Proud of her retrieve, Daisey carried the big drake with her head high and at a fast trot. I wondered how many more years she could take this physical abuse and, at the end of the same thought, how many years I might have left.

Funny how your mind wanders. I remembered my friend Bill Whitson, a dedicated duck shooter. One cold day in December, while the rest of his party went into the cabin for lunch, Bill stayed in the blind. When they returned, they found Bill dead from a heart attack. A fine way to go, but I wasn't ready yet!

My second drake mallard accompanied a flock of six blacks. They flew in low, just over the water, saw the stools, and almost tore the feathers off their wings fighting their way into the near gale force wind. They looked the size of geese until I sat up and they flared. I fired twice and never came near the mallard. The second shot was a waste of a shell as the wind carried the flaring birds out of range in an instant. My lead was off; the strong wind and forward speed of the birds had changed conditions radically and I was not taking this into account.

When the next mallard came over the decoys at thirty yards, I swung through the bird, and kept the gun moving even further ahead of the bird than I thought was necessary before pulling the trigger. The duck fell dead. I had found the formula. The mallard landed outside of the decoys with one wing stuck up in the air, causing the bird to sail with the wind. Daisey ran along the edge of the marsh bank and when she was parallel with the drifting duck, she dove in and intercepted the bird.

While she was bringing in the bird, I recalled how a judge in a field trial had marked down my old Labrador, Cindy, when she did this same thing on a long, marked fall. The dog's idea is to get the bird, and get back as quickly as possible. Some field trial judges don't always see it that way.

My third mallard arrived with a flock of several black ducks just as snow began to fall. This was no ordinary snowfall, but one of those storms that blows at you horizontally; one side of your body may have half an inch of snow on it before the other side gets wet. I lost the location of the mallard in the confusion over the decoys and didn't see the drake again till I sat up to shoot. The mallard flared and laid back on the wind. In desperation I threw the muzzle past the bird and fired. The mallard appeared to be only wing-tipped and sailed toward the open water of the bay.

I shouldn't have sent the dog, but I did. She disappeared into the snow in pursuit of a very lively, swimming duck that was being aided by a strong tail wind. I cussed myself for risking Daisey under these conditions. She could easily get lost or confused in this snowstorm and lose track of the location of the shoreline. I ran to the sneakbox, started the motor, and headed downwind, looking for her. I felt myself panicking when I was a hundred yards from the decoys and didn't see her.

Then, there she was, mallard-in-mouth, swimming hard against the seas toward me. I cut the engine, grabbed her by the scruff of the neck, and hauled her into the cockpit of the sneakbox. She had been in the rough water for twenty minutes, fighting it all the way. What wonderful animals, these Labradors. At that moment, I felt honored to have a dog that was bred to hunt and knows how to do it.

Back at the coffin, Daisey curled up in her eelgrass nest as I stomped around to get warm, then dug out another pair of gloves and a heavy wool sweater. The temperature was plummeting. Ice was freezing on my jacket and the decoys were glazed over—a few were half-sunk from the weight of the ice. I knew that our gunning time was slipping away.

Trying to identify my last mallard in the snowstorm was next to impossible. I must have let fifty black ducks pass before I glimpsed a light-colored duck that might have been a mallard, but wasn't a black duck. I never took my eye off the bird until the flock had set up over the decoys. My first shot was a miss; the second hit the bird, which sailed out over the marsh and landed in high grass. Daisey marked the area of the fall, but I didn't think she would find the bird given the storm's severity and the poor scenting conditions.

By now, the weather had worsened, and quitting time was only an hour away. I unloaded the gun, stowed my gear, and was wading out to pick up the decoys when Daisey delivered the hen mallard. That rounded out my limit, and I was more than ready to head back to the houseboat to get warm.

It was a downwind run to the shack where the wood stove had the place cozy-warm. The indoor-outdoor thermometer read seventy-five inside and five degrees outdoors. The wind chill factor had to be around minus twenty-five degrees. As my hands and cheeks began to warm, they stung and burned. Steam rose off Daisey as she curled near the warm wood stove.

I figured that by leaving immediately we could return to the landing through the snowstorm and strong wind before dark. On the other hand, I calculated that if we had engine problems, broke a shear pin, or took on too much ice, we would be overtaken by darkness—not a good scenario. Daylight is your best friend during the winter.

I called my wife on the citizen's band radio. She agreed that we should stay the night, but asked us to be home by present-opening time on Christmas morning. This was no problem.

For dinner that Christmas Eve, I filleted out the breasts of two of the fattest mallards, fried some potatoes and onions, opened a can of peas, made some biscuits, and set two places at the table. It was like having a guest for dinner, except Daisey ate her meal on the floor.

By eight o'clock the outside temperature was zero. After loading the wood stove with oak logs, I blocked off the door to one room of the gunning shack with a blanket to concentrate the heat. Then, I made the convertible sofa into a double bed. I laid a couple of blankets under the bottom sheet and piled two on top. In bed I could feel Daisey's heavy body against my feet, and I cherished this moment of companionship after a fine, but hard day of teamwork. Within moments, Daisey and I fell asleep with the wind howling and the shack rocking on its cedar pilings, far out on a tidal marsh in Barnegat Bay on Christmas Eve.

CHAPTER SEVENTEEN

Matters of the Heart
By Chris Cornell

Tough times are part of owning a good Labrador retriever—like the frustration of having to give up on a crippled duck after a half-hour of handling. Or watching your dog perform near-perfect triple marks and double blind retrieves in a hunt test, only to see him break instead of honoring the next dog's work.

Then there are the truly sad and ominous moments, like hearing him yelp in pain when his arthritic elbows give out as he tries to climb a steep bank. Or noticing that he no longer streaks back from long retrieves; he trots, because running is too painful. It's when the muzzle that rests on your knee is not the solid black of youth, but the mottled white of age. It's when you realize that you have to give up the competitive tests and trials you both love so much. It's when you are forced to admit that the days your dog can handle the physical demands of a long duck hunt are numbered.

And so it was during a November not long past that I found myself in the back seat of a Suburban, skimming through fog-shrouded Missouri farmland with my nine-year-old Lab, Tad, behind me in his crate, sleeping off the excitement of his first plane flight. Months before, I had decided that if Tad had to be retired, we were going to have one last, great hunt together. And it wouldn't be our typical sojourn to the Mill Pond, or the Gig, or the St. George River in Maine, where he'd be lucky to get three or four retrieves for the day. No, this was going to be the real thing—a hunt on the Mississippi Flyway for the mallards that each fall flock to America's heartland by the tens of thousands to feed in the corn and soybean fields that were now whizzing past the car window.

• • •

Guide Leon Holcomb's quiet, "Here we go, boys" was followed by a perfect, staccato highball that he threw at three birds clearing the tree line a quarter-mile to our left. Tad was sitting outside the pit blind and picked up the ducks immediately. His ears cocked high on his broad head while he listened to Leon's insistent calling, and his eyes tracked the mallards as they turned toward us. On the first pass over the decoys, the birds were too high. My shooting partner, Ralph Stuart, and I fought the temptation to look up as they swung over the winter rye behind us. Leon switched the cadence and volume of his calling, pleading with the ducks to drop into the dekes, working to convince them it was where they wanted to be.

On their second pass—lower, and directly in front—Leon said, "Take 'em." A hen scaled away, dead, sixty yards to the right; a bright-headed drake splashed down twenty yards to our front. I offered the dog—and myself—silent congratulations that he stayed rock-steady during the shooting. Tad's eyes were locked on the drake, the last bird down, when I sent him. Lunging through shallows at first, then swimming in deeper water, he made quick, stylish work of the retrieve and delivered the big mallard to hand. Would he remember the hen? I asked myself. I should have had faith in my dog—he was already lined up on the hen's fall as he sat to deliver the drake.

"Fetch!" and he was off again, arrowing through the dekes and the stalks of corn and millet that had proved too much of a temptation for the ducks. Returning with the hen, Tad barely acknowledged my "Good boy!" and pat on the head. He was already looking out over the decoys, waiting for the next birds. Everything felt just right.

Between flurries of action, we watched as huge, densely packed flocks of red-winged blackbirds wheeled and dipped over the standing corn to our left; the *whoosh* of their collective wings punctuated a kaleidoscopic display of synchronized aerobatics. Above them, two red-tailed hawks rode the morning's thermals and occasionally dive-bombed the blackbirds, to no avail. High-pitched honks in the azure sky announced long, ragged Vs of snow geese flying toward some invisible, predetermined destination; their white bodies and wings flashed in the late-morning sun. A large deer picked its way through an oak stand on the far side of the cornfield.

My Labrador, of course, was unimpressed by these sights and sounds. He was there for one reason only—ducks—and they suddenly appeared out of nowhere, three tightly bunched drakes that shocked us from our mid-morning reverie. All three of us promptly blasted holes in the sky, and I muttered something about Ralph's "near-legendary" shooting skills while we endured Tad's icy stare.

Then, for what seemed like an eternity, Leon worked his call on a pair of mallards that swung over, high, for a look at our spread. They circled twice, interested but not seduced, and I began to wonder when Leon was going to run out of air. Ralph took matters into his own hands, made a long overhead shot, and dropped one of the birds into the decoys. When the second duck swung in back of the blind, I followed suit, and cartwheeled it into the winter rye fifty yards behind us.

Tad made quick work of both birds. The marking ability that was bred into him—always his strong suit—made me look good, though beyond refining that innate talent, I had little to do with it. As he delivered the second mallard, there were grins all around. And this time, my praise of the dog even elicited some mild tail-wagging.

An hour later, we had half a day's limit and decided to head to the lodge. Leon fetched the truck and helped me lift my wet and tired ninety-pound Labrador over the tailgate. Tad was stiff, but content.

• • •

Days had passed in a figurative heartbeat, and it was our last afternoon of hunting in the heartland. The morning's outing had been a bust, so Leon was feeling pressure, though Ralph and I told him not to worry. We set up in a new spot called the Round Hole, a circular pocket of water deep in the flooded corn. The sky was sunny and clear, but a rising wind rustled the dry stalks around us, bolstering our hopes that the birds would fly.

Tad was feeling the effects of two and a half days of hard hunting. He limped badly in the mornings, due not so much to his arthritic elbows but to some mysterious injury to his left front foot. I worried that a sliver of cornstalk had been driven up under a toenail, but repeated examinations showed nothing. Thankfully, the cold mud of the flooded fields seemed to provide some relief. Although I agonized over whether or not to leave Tad behind, I knew he had to be with me on that last afternoon.

As we waited in the pit, the dog was perched just outside, on an impossibly small mound of mud. He was restless, scanning the empty skies and talking deep in his throat, nudging me persistently with his white muzzle. This time, I couldn't bring myself to discipline him, so I just scratched his broad chest in the calming rhythm that seems to soothe all dogs.

That's what I was doing when two mallards screamed in low over the corn and took us by surprise. We dropped both, and the dog made a quick job of the double. Minutes later, Leon pulled in another bunch, and Ralph knocked down a drake in front of us. While the dog swam for it, three more birds swung behind us, and Leon dumped one far back in the corn.

I climbed out of the pit, took Ralph's duck from the dog, and splashed around the back side of the pit to send Tad on the blind retrieve of Leon's bird. Once he entered the corn, handling would be impossible, so I hoped my initial line was right. It was, and the dog arrived back at my side in short order. As we approached the pit, more birds swung in, and I dropped to my knees in the muck, hissing at the dog to sit. I watched one drake flare and tumble, then there were more shots and splashes of birds the dog and I couldn't see from behind the blind.

"Three down," Leon told me as I stood up and sent Tad for the bird he had marked. Moving out front to take the duck, I heeled the dog in tight on the little mound of mud and asked about the location of the other falls. A dead drake, a slim glimmer of emerald in the low sun, was floating thirty yards away, in the edge of the corn on the opposite side of the Round Hole. We tackled that first, and the dog needed just one left-hand *Over!* to put him on the bird.

The third duck in the triple was hidden and required Tad to push through a bunch of cornstalks in front of us, cross open water, and make an angled entry into the main body of standing corn. He took and held the line I gave him, but after several minutes, he swam out of the cover empty-mouthed.

"That line looked good," Leon said, so I gave the dog a left-hand over and sent him into the corn again. Once more, Tad appeared without the bird. By that time I was frustrated, and no doubt, so was my dog.

I whistled him in and set him up again on a slightly different angle, a bit more to the left. Tad accepted the subtle adjustment and drove out on the new line, into the corn. This time, I heard the familiar snuffling that meant he had the bird, and as he swam back to me, I felt a burst of pride. Though Tad had done hundreds of combination triple marks and double blinds in training and trials, these were his first such retrieves in the field—exactly the reason why we were in the heartland.

The dog and I settled back into position. There were more birds, more shots, more retrieves. The rhythm of swinging the gun barrel through each duck as I fired came naturally on this third day of hunting; I was shooting as well as I ever had. Tad was all business, too, waiting silently, and handling marks and blind retrieves with equal skill. It was the best duck hunting day we had known as a team.

When our watches told us that it was time to unload the guns and head back to the vehicles, we clambered reluctantly out of the pit. Then it was a matter of shouldering the gear, slogging back through the flooded corn, and walking into the fading shadows of the oak trees, their dry, brown leaves still resisting late fall's chilling frosts and tugging breezes.

Predictably, to the ducks the end of legal shooting hours was the signal to fly in earnest. As I stood next to Leon's truck, I saw them pouring out of the nearby lake into the corn we had just left. Singles, doubles, groups of three and five and eight rose to tree-top level, then swung around and headed for the feedlot Leon had created for them. Against melded hues of purple, pink, blue, and orange in the western sky they came, talking to each other, banking, setting wings, dumping air, and dropping in as only hungry ducks sure of their safety can.

My big Labrador, tired but still very much alert, seemed to

sense that something special was happening. Without my saying a word, he sat and watched silently as the now windless sky filled with the ducks that defined who he was and what he did. Now, there were no whines of anticipation, no trembles of excitement; just an extraordinary calm that perfectly matched the moment— and my own mood.

Quietly, I edged to Leon's side and asked if we could stay for the evening show—just for a few minutes? His broad smile was the perfect answer. I moved ten feet down the slope, to Tad's side. Together, in a place and in a way that we'd never been together before, we listened and looked at our dream: hundreds of mallards, silhouetted against the darkening sky. The birds that were already on the water conversed in the feeding gabble that I've never been able to master on a call. Other ducks, just landed, called to their more reluctant brethren in the long, loud, insistent come-back sequence that Leon had duplicated so often and so perfectly in the three days of our hunt.

Side by side, Tad and I soaked up each sight and sound the way dry grass absorbs a summer rain. As his blocky head swung to follow groups of wheeling ducks, I knelt next to him and put my hand gently on the back of his neck, feeling the thick fur and heavy muscles that had served him so well for so long.

As we watched the birds in the fading light, I tried not to think about the hard truth that he and I, together, would never see this sight again. And I succeeded—because sometimes, just sometimes, once is so good that once is enough.

CHAPTER EIGHTEEN

Yellow Dog
By E. Donnall Thomas, Jr.

There aren't a lot of rules in the business of outdoor writing, but here are two of them: Don't write about dead friends or dead dogs. Having willfully disregarded the first of these tenets, I see no reason to treat the second as inviolate.

The arrival of Skykomish Sunka Zee into our lives came heavily flavored with circumstance. My wife, Susan, and I were in Seattle visiting our families when our friends Dick and Ray called from Montana to tell us that our Lab had been struck by a car and killed. The news was devastating. Never mind that the deceased had been a hardheaded, ill-mannered, pain-in-the-ass by all objective criteria. We had no kids then and our dog occupied the affection receptors in the emotional part of the brain ordinarily reserved for one's children.

By unstated agreement, Dick, Ray, and I have never discussed the details of that dog's death, although I inferred that one of them was at the wheel of the lethal vehicle. After watching me endure several seasons of apoplexy at the hands of the dog, it is even possible that they took advantage of my absence to do me one of the biggest favors of my life. Twenty years after the fact, I don't know and I don't want to know.

But there I was, stranded in Seattle with no hunting dog in my life for the first time ever. My father offered his sympathy. (I now suspect he secretly rejoiced in the knowledge that he would not have to hunt with that dog again the following season.)

Then he gave me some simple advice: Go find another one. So I did.

There are many theories governing the selection of puppies, most emphasizing a careful analysis of papers and scrutiny of the sire and dam. I didn't have time for any of that. After answering a couple of ads in the paper, I drove out to a farm on the edge of the city and talked to the owners of what sounded like the most promising litter. They impressed me as good people. The dog's papers were in order. Without further ado, I reached down into the wriggling mass of yellow puppies and, in one of the great triumphs of dumb luck, withdrew, at random, what turned out to be the best hunting dog I have ever trained.

Susan and I had taken to naming dogs after our favorite steelhead streams and decided at first to call this one Skykomish Sunrise, after both the river and the steelhead pattern that originated there. Evidently, another enthusiast of steelhead and Labrador retrievers had thought of the same thing, because the AKC bounced that one right back at us. We were living on the Fort Peck Reservation at the time, and while my spoken Sioux was scarcely adequate to find trouble on Saturday night, an elderly Indian friend was able to help me with the translation of yellow dog, and the puppy became Skykomish Sunka Zee.

We lived a long way from the distractions of clear-water trout streams then, and the growing dog enjoyed plenty of attention that summer. By the time bird season approached, it was apparent that Sky was highly precocious. He marked and handled and hunted with plenty of puppy enthusiasm, but remarkably little puppy silliness. The obvious question was what to do with this developing prodigy come September?

The dog would be nine months old when bird season opened. There is plenty of opportunity to ruin a dog that age by exposing him to the noise and confusion of the hunt before he is emotionally mature enough for the experience. All young dogs do things in the field that need to be discouraged. If the dog associates the discouragement with the hunt itself rather than the specific infraction, potential may be lost forever.

On the other hand, the best students deserve to be challenged, whether they are adolescent dogs or adolescent children. I tried not to let myself be influenced too much by the fact that nine-month-old Sky was now the only dog I had, and that the thought of spending an autumn in eastern Montana without a bird dog was nearly unbearable. That was *my* problem, I told myself, and I had no business compromising a good young dog just because I needed to go hunting.

Then opening day rolled around, and I took him hunting anyway. In retrospect, the decision makes me look like a dog training genius.

On the morning of the first Saturday in September, Dick and I walked down into a grassy swale somewhere in the middle of the prairie with Sky and Dick's setter bouncing along happily in front of us. Several hundred yards later, I crested a little rise to find Sky locked solidly on point in front of me. The sight of a Labrador retriever frozen into a comical parody of a pointing dog stopped me squarely in my tracks.

"You're not going to believe this!" I yelled over to Dick, and when he walked across the draw to join us, he confirmed that he did not. Finally, we recovered from the apparent absurdity of the situation long enough to walk in and flush the covey of sage hens and drop three or four of them, at which point the dog was free to be a retriever once more.

This is not a story about pointing Labs, although for the rest of his career, Sky repeated this performance just often enough to let me know that it was no accident. He pointed once or twice a year for reasons that were never clear or predictable, and when he did, he seemed to do so passively, as if the point was a phenomenon totally beyond his control that left him every bit as mystified as it left us. If that first, glorious demonstration really meant anything more than a few dead birds, it was simply that hunting with Skykomish Sunka Zee was never likely to be boring—and sure enough, it never was.

We enjoyed quite a rookie season together. At first, I promised myself we would stick to sharptails and sage hens because they are easy on young dogs and their pursuit minimizes the need for discipline. However, as waterfowl season approached, it was obvious that the dog was ready for ducks—he took to the water like an otter. By the time we left the blind on opening day, he had proven himself.

Pheasant hunting is the graduate school of dog work for the versatile retriever, but by the end of October I sensed that he was ready. The high plains ringnecks taught him a lesson or two, but he took his lumps in sporting fashion and brought enough birds to hand to establish both his confidence in himself and my confidence in him.

It was his second season, however, that confirmed the fact that we were beyond the fast-learner category and into the realm of the exceptional.

During the first week of October, we were hunting sharptails and Huns in a broad expanse of prairie surrounding a shallow, man-made lake. The entire lake has since gone dry, but at the time it was one of the largest bodies of water around, measuring several miles across. It usually contained plenty of waterfowl, but there was almost no cover around its edges, and most of the ducks would raft up in the middle where they were all but impossible to hunt.

A broad earthen dam rimmed the western edge of the lake, and as I walked back toward the truck, I decided to climb over the top just to see what was there. As luck would have it, a flock of teal was resting right behind the dam. It was a long shot from the top of the dam to the waterline, but as the teal flushed, I swung on the nearest bird and broke the tip of its wing.

The teal splashed back down into the water and began to

swim. The surface of the lake was calm and the dog marked the fall easily. When I released him from my side, he hit the water with a great geyser of spray and I settled down in the sagebrush to watch the show.

Puddle ducks with broken wingtips usually lower their profiles and swim for cover onshore, where they have the best chance of eluding pursuers. Perhaps this bird knew enough to distrust the barren shoreline, for it headed straight toward the middle of the lake with the dog paddling furiously behind. Teal are surprisingly strong swimmers, and with the substantial head start that the long shot provided, it was apparent that Sky had an epic retrieve in front of him.

I considered whistling the dog back, but losing a cripple is enough to ruin any day and calling an enthusiastic retriever off a retrieve seems like a violation of natural order. As the gap between the teal and the dog started to close relentlessly, the duck began to dive. They were several hundred yards from shore by this time, and I assumed that Sky would eventually lose the trail out there in the open water and return to shore. Little did I know.

It was a bright, sunny afternoon and the surface of the lake shimmered like a mirage in the distance. I soon lost sight of the bird entirely, and then the dog's head got smaller and smaller as he circled farther away across the water. Finally, I lost sight of him as well.

Few places on earth feel quite as empty as a calm, flat lake in the middle of the prairie, especially when it has consumed your favorite hunting dog. As ridiculous as the situation felt, there was really nothing to do but wait; and so I waited. For an hour and a half, by the watch.

Shadows were lengthening behind the dam by the time a tiny dot appeared upon the lake's indistinct horizon. It is hard to tell about small, distant objects across large reaches of open water. Study the sea long enough and you can imagine all kinds of things out there. Every time I do it, I appreciate why whaling captains sent their very best eyes aloft to the crow's nest. After staring intently and looking away and staring again, I convinced myself that the object was more than the product of wishful thinking, that it was getting steadily larger, and finally, that it really was my dog returning to port.

I stood and whistled and waved my arms to give him a point of reference against the background of light in the western sky. The whistle's trill rolled away across the water and then I could hear the dog's swimming noise answer me, a high-pitched sound like a goldeneye in flight that in the years to come would define his enthusiasm for water retrieves. Finally, he got some ground beneath his feet and bounded up out of the water. We met halfway between the dam and the waterline. The teal was resting quietly in his mouth with its dark eye still alert and its plumage unruffled, as if it had merely hitched a ride across the lake.

That was the moment I realized that the next years of my life were going to be special, just as the parents of a musical or athletic prodigy eventually realize that without intending to do so, they have become involved in something that may be larger than themselves.

• • •

Ray and I were standing in a blind next to a prairie pothole later that season when we got our first look at another of Sky's unique abilities. Once again, it was not immediately clear that he was going to survive the strength of his own character.

A set of mallards had come into the decoys and we both doubled easily. Three of the birds were stone-dead and Sky and Ray's Chessie had them in our hands in short order. The fourth bird was a problem. It had a broken wing, and nothing challenges a dog quite like a mature mallard with everything still working except its flight apparatus.

I suspect there are complex rules of engagement that are supposed to apply to these situations, but our own rules are simple: We want our cripples in our hands as quickly and cleanly as possible, and it doesn't matter what dog gets the job done.

I had kept my eye on the last duck, which was heading for the opposite shore in its stealth mode, with nothing but its snout visible above the water. We lined out both dogs and sent them. After a minute or so of pursuit, they had the bird surrounded. Then the mallard sounded, as wounded mallards predictably will. Unable to see or smell the submerged duck, Ray's Chessie thrashed about the water frantically. Sky, on the other hand, dove right along with the bird.

At first we assumed that he had simply ducked underwater in an attempt to grab the mallard as it swam past him, but he failed to surface. Ray expressed his bewilderment. I began to fret, imagining all sorts of underwater mishaps that might befall a dog. Finally, a boil appeared on the brown water like a whale breaching, and there was Sky, a good twenty yards from the spot where he had disappeared. And yes, he held the mallard firmly but gently in his mouth.

Years later, I learned of a professional trainer who tried to teach retrievers to dive in the pursuit of swimming ducks. He used an elaborate system of pulleys to draw training dummies progressively deeper under water, and claimed some success in getting his dogs to perform this spectacular maneuver. Based on years of experience with Sky, I can only say that the result is well worth some effort if you appreciate dramatic retrieves, and that it's a hell of a lot easier to get the job done if you start with a dog who knows the trick in the first place.

The underwater retrieve became one of Sky's signature techniques, and he performed it with such mastery that I always wished we could name it for him, like a Sukahara on the rings or an Immelmann in the air. It was not just a matter of putting his head underwater to take a swipe at a duck as if he were bobbing for apples. He went down, like a submarine, and when something had to come up for air, it was almost always the duck. First-time observers invariably gasped as the seconds ticked by, while those of us who knew Sky waited patiently, confident that something amazing was in progress right before our eyes.

I had two more years of medical training to get out of the way, so Sky spent his third and fourth seasons in Seattle rather than the bird-rich environment of the Montana prairie. All was not lost, however. The University of Washington was developing rural medical training programs around the Northwest, and, protesting like B'rer Rabbit on the edge of the briar patch, I volunteered to spend both autumns of my internal medicine residency back in Montana on assignments no one else wanted. And once we were back in the bird cover, Sky acted as if we had never left.

I returned to eastern Montana as soon as possible, and during the years that followed, Sky performed at his absolute prime. In the late 70s, the drought had not yet impacted prairie duck populations, and Hun and sharptail numbers were at their peak. It is difficult to imagine that any dog in America had more wild birds of more species shot over him than Sky during that period of time. He was still young enough to hunt all day, but experienced enough to know what he was doing, and I suppose the same can be said for those of us who hunted with him.

Ray handled some good Chessies then, and an amicable inter-service rivalry developed between us on behalf of our dogs, culminating in the nearly mystical tradition of the Retrieve of the Year honor. No matter how dramatic the Chessies' water entries or how stalwart they were in the face of cold, Sky always managed to do something so amazing that the Retrieve of the Year became his personal province. Chesapeake Bay retriever chauvinist that he was—and always will be—even Ray had to admit that Sky was the dog of a lifetime.

Of course, even the greatest dogs have their faults and Sky was no exception. In fact, he had two peculiar habits that threatened to drive me crazy until I learned to put them both in perspective.

The first was a tendency to become psychotic under high

wind conditions. One day early in his second season, we were walking back to our truck in a real prairie howler. A covey of Huns rose at the edge of a stubble field and I somehow managed to double in spite of the gale. Both birds were stone-dead in the open, forty yards upwind of us, and it looked like an absolutely routine retrieve. Halfway to the birds, the dog stopped with the air breaking around him like water in a trout stream and refused to advance farther. He tacked back and forth across the swirling current with his nose held high, trying to decipher the torrent of scent. He just couldn't do it. His guidance systems had come undone. I watched him work back and forth aimlessly for ten or fifteen minutes before I walked out into the stubble and showed him the birds. Even then, he acted as if he didn't believe they were real.

We watched him repeat that performance once or twice each season, always when working into brisk, swirling wind. Dogs commonly have problems under such conditions, but they reduced Sky to utter helplessness. I think that his nose was just so good that he didn't know what to do when it misled him.

His second fault was even stranger. Despite having one of the softest mouths of any dog I have ever hunted with, Sky could not let a season pass without eating one bird. And I do mean eat. I never saw him romp with a bird, or hard-mouth one. Of the untold number of birds and ducks that he retrieved for me over the years, I cannot remember one arriving at hand with a puncture wound courtesy of the dog. But once a season he would select a bird from the vast number at his disposal and devour it.

These transgressions never seemed to correlate with anything. Sometimes it would be a duck, sometimes a grouse, sometimes a pheasant. The dog was always well fed and the offenses took place under a wide variety of hunting conditions. It seemed to be something that he just could not help doing.

He did it for the first time during his puppy season. I dismissed the offense as youthful indiscretion and, in accordance with my promises to myself, I didn't come down on him too hard. When he repeated the same crime during his derby year, however, he obviously knew better, as confirmed by the painfully guilty look on his feather-coated face when I happened upon the scene of the crime. His grace period was over, and I got after him about as hard as I ever got after him for anything. He took his licks bravely and without resentment, as always, and for the rest of the season, he treated the birds in his mouth the way a mother would treat a newborn baby.

It took me two more seasons to accept the fact that he was going to eat a bird now and then no matter what I did. I simply hoped that he would have the courtesy to do it when we were alone, rather than in the company of friends. Of course, it didn't always work out that way. During one of my medical residency years, my father stopped in Billings for a quick weekend of bird hunting. We drove south into unfamiliar country and spent all day hiking through cactus containing some of the biggest rattlesnakes I have ever seen in my life. After hours in the rising heat, we finally jumped a small covey of Huns and he dropped one, at which point we decided to retreat before the snakes ate us.

On the way home, we pulled into a cafe to rehydrate, and when we came out, the truck was awash in feathers. Ten man-hours of labor had disappeared down the gullet of a Labrador retriever. There wasn't anything left but to head for home and a bottle of bourbon to contemplate the meaning of it all.

In time, I gave up and stopped punishing him physically for these once-a-year exercises in delinquency. I always disliked whacking him anyway, and it clearly wasn't doing any good. When I caught him in the act, I would sit him down with what evidence I could muster. Then I would kneel on the ground in front of him and stare him in the eye until he could not stand the burden of his sins any longer. Finally, I would get in his face and snarl, *"You shit-head!"* with as much dramatic contempt as I could manage, and when he looked away in misery we would be done with it for the year.

Sky was seven years old when my wife and I moved to Alaska. We had kids of our own by then (kids without floppy ears and long tails, that is), but the detachment that developed between my kennel and me had nothing to do with sibling competition. Bird hunting in the far north is a bit of a stretch, at least if you are accustomed to the plains of eastern Montana. However, Alaska is every bowhunter's dream, so for several years I spent most of my free time during hunting season with my longbow in pursuit of sheep and moose and caribou. Sky took all this in stride because he was a gentleman. But he never failed to display enthusiasm when given a chance, and many of my ptarmigan hunts and ritual trips to the Duck Shack were made largely for his benefit.

173

November is a grim month in south central Alaska, especially for an outdoorsman accustomed to looking forward to November all year long. After a season or two of trying desperately to conjure up some kind of outdoor sport from the cold and dark, I got smart and made a return trip to my Montana roots part of my regular November itinerary. We would stay at Ray's and hunt pheasants in the morning and whitetails in the evening, and no matter how cold it became in our tree stands, I sensed that there was no better place on earth to be.

Sky went with me, of course. Transporting a dog through the world's airline system is one of life's great hassles, and one in which, despite the well-known business maxim to the contrary, the customer is always wrong. On every one of those trips, I reached the point of screaming in rage at various airline bean counters over some stupid rule governing the transport of Labrador retrievers from Alaska to Montana and back, but there really wasn't much to be done about it. I wasn't going to Montana in November without a bird dog, especially that bird dog. Period.

On our third such excursion, we spent the first day hunting pheasants from dawn until dark. The weather had been dry and that was the first of several poor upland bird seasons in a row, but my own legs were full of spring from months of hard hunting in Alaska and it didn't bother anyone that we had to work hard for our birds. Sky looked tired that night and I hand-fed him an extra ration of something nutritious. The following morning, he was a bit less bouncy than usual but he still seemed eager to go. We found more birds that day and limited by noon. I put the dog in

Ray's kennel to rest up a bit and then we set off to hunt whitetails.

That evening, I went out to feed the dogs and discovered that Sky wouldn't stand up. I could not find anything specific wrong with him, and it took me a long, sleepless night to realize that he wasn't sick at all. There hadn't been enough bird hunting in Alaska to reveal the obvious, but a day and a half on the prairie had left him no room to hide. The simple fact was that he had grown old.

From then on, hunting with Sky was largely a matter of ceremony. We moved back to Montana the following year, and he survived the trip without ill effect. I took him out a time or two that fall and let him snuffle around in the bird cover, but that was about all he could manage. It was obvious that he had made his last water retrieve and, by the end of the season, it was obvious that he had made his last bird hunt as well.

One tragedy of great dogs is that their very greatness makes it all but impossible to groom their replacements. I had brought several pups along during the years I hunted with Sky, but none of them seemed to show any real promise, perhaps because my own notion of promise had been hopelessly skewed by the dog already waiting to go whenever I wanted to hunt birds. Those pups all wound up as potlickers or kids' dogs or refugees in good country homes. Perhaps if I had worked a little longer or a little harder with one or two of them . . . Who knows?

The second tragedy of great dogs is that due to the inner workings of our various biological clocks, we will almost always outlive them. When that happens, you can expect an emptiness to appear where vitality and enthusiasm once reigned, and that emptiness is never easy to reconcile. That's what happened the first spring after our return from Alaska, when Sky walked out in the yard one day and lay down and died. The fact that each of us can only hope for an equally serene end was little consolation at first. I missed my dog, and not just because I would never shoot as many birds without him. I missed him because he defined one segment of my life, and now that chapter was over.

Life does go on, however. With no impossible standard left to compromise the process, I reached into another squirming litter of puppies, closed my eyes, and grabbed. I tried to remember the smell of the barn on the outskirts of Seattle and the way I let my fingers run across all those wriggling bodies, and I tried to do everything the same way, just as a gambler will try to throw the dice the same way he did when he hit the biggest numbers of his life.

Luck prevailed. I picked Sonny. He promises to be another story someday, and I can imagine no more elegant ending to a tale about a Labrador retriever that brought a special sense of meaning to my life.

CHAPTER NINETEEN

Obligations
By Steve Wright

Putting down an old dog is a hard thing to do—much like, I imagine, authorizing a doctor to shut down the life-support systems of a dying relative. I remember watching my tired, old Labrador in the middle of the living room floor and thinking these same thoughts. He had been my first dog, but I knew this segment of my life was coming to a close.

I first saw him as a pup rolling around behind a wire enclosure in a dimly lit Georgia barn. When I poked my finger through the wire, he released a choke hold on a littermate, came bounding over, seized my finger, and sliced it open with a needle-sharp canine. "That's the one I want," I said to the breeder while cradling the bleeding finger in a handkerchief.

My wife and I were young then, newly married and filled with fascination for each other. We brought him home in February and lavished attention on him. We did not make love for weeks, and I recall thinking then how odd that the dog could have that effect on us. We poured our emotion and attention into him. He was our first child.

One day, while talking dogs with one of my older and wiser professors, I was told, "Get James Lamb Free's book, and use it to train that dog and any children you might have." I had grown up with pointing dogs, but had never trained an animal—except for a few unsuccessful attempts on my younger brothers. I bought the book and followed it religiously.

We made it through most of the lessons—through the hand signals part, anyway—and I was pretty proud. Some days we would go over to the university recreation fields and show off for the sorority girls.

I began hunting him after his first year—a mistake, some said. But he seemed capable, and I was impatient. His first retrieve was a dove at a local shoot. He spat it out at my feet and looked up, feathers covering his tongue and muzzle, with eyes that said, "I'm not so sure about this." He spent the next ten minutes gagging, but never once hesitated on a retrieve.

I made one fundamental training error. I did not steady him to wing and shot. In his thirteen-year career, this was a significant annoyance. The embarrassing fault became apparent during his first season, mostly at dove shoots before substantial audiences. I took him back through the basics. No luck. I tried to force it into him. No luck. Whenever the gun went off, so did the dog—in the general direction I had fired. I decided to try trickery. The reasoning seemed sound: He was strong—but not too strong for a parachute cord—and coming to an abrupt end-over-end stop should do the trick. Sure, several repetitions might be necessary. I wasn't worried.

We drove out to a recently plowed-in cornfield. The neat furrows of red Georgia clay smelled good, and there were a few doves around picking at scattered kernels. I retreated into the brush at the edge of the field and sat the dog. I snapped twenty feet of parachute cord to his leather collar, tied the loose end around my waist, and waited for a dove to come along. I was about to settle the shot-breaking habit for keeps.

It didn't take long. Two doves drifted past with that distinctive honey-stirring movement of their wings. The dog saw them. I said *Mark*, then fired and missed—not unusual. The dog broke shot—not unusual either. Nearly thirty years later I can still see the line paying out, the coils springing to life like a rattlesnake. I can even recall the thought racing through my mind: *Now I'm gonna settle this*, a little grin on my lips.

I am still relieved that no other hunters were around that field. The sight of a human body catapulted from the brush would have brought them running. With the dog about halfway out, I was on my feet, heels set. I yelled "Whoa," just before he hit the end of the rope—and that's when I was catapulted from cover along the edge of the field. For an instant, I felt like a kite towed by a kid at the park. Then gravity took over and I nosed into a red-clay furrow. But I did not stop moving. This black locomotive was dragging me across the plowed field, pursuing two fleeing doves that seemed to be looking back over their wings in terror at the thing chasing them. I was not quick enough to get to my feet between lunges, and could only rise to a point where I was thrown forward to extract another bite from the next furrow.

179

I was well acquainted with the principles of biology and physics and knew this could not continue, but what would be the limiting factor? Would the dog simply tire? Would he sense that the weight he was pulling and the screams he was presumably hearing were related, and pause to look back and ascertain their origin? Would he continue his churning as long as he could see the two doves and, if so, was this then a test of his visual acuity? And what if another dove or even a sapsucker intersected our course? Would we begin anew at a ninety-degree angle? The thought occurred to me that if he did turn ninety degrees, at least I would be dragged in the direction of the furrows and not have to eat so much red clay.

And then he stopped and looked back. He was a little winded, but not breathing too hard. He seemed surprised to see me there, twenty feet away. He seemed to be thinking, "Oh, hi boss. What are you doing here? I thought you were back there in the brush. Do you know you missed those two doves? They went over there, over those big pine trees. Too bad. Let's do it again."

I had red clay from head to foot. I had red clay in my hair, my eyes, my mouth, my navel, and my underwear. My pockets were full of red clay. Fortunately, my shotgun was still on the edge of the field. I wobbled to my feet, walked over to the dog, and snapped the parachute cord off his collar.

With head down, I stumbled back across the furrows, picked up my shotgun, and walked back to the car with the dog at heel, his tongue lolling. I put the dog in the car, got behind the wheel—sifting red clay over the seat covers—and drove home. I never again tried to break him of that habit. Instead, I just yelled a lot.

A short time after the furrow incident, we all moved to Vermont—my wife, the dog, and a new six-month-old son. We made the trip in the cab of a U-Haul—all four of us—north to the promised land. I was looking for wild country, and I found it in the Northeast Kingdom—a three-county area of northern Vermont jammed up against Quebec and New Hampshire. As Aldo Leopold once remarked about another place, "It was poor land but good country."

The dog was suited to Vermont. He was tough and businesslike. And he was a good protector. Another son joined the family, and the dog adopted both boys in spite of the incessant tail-pulling and ear-chewing. He was their security blanket.

We learned to hunt grouse and woodcock, and the dog stayed close—except when the gun went off. We hunted black ducks, woodies, mallards, and teal, with skim ice in the cattails and on the beaver ponds. He never failed me.

He would retrieve anything. Bury an arrow in the grass? No problem, call the dog. A foul ball out of play and into the brush? Call the dog. Lost your wallet? Call the dog. Wounded deer? Call the dog. Once, on a fishing trip to Idaho, I broke off my last Muddler with a sloppy backcast. I called the dog, opened my streamer wallet, let him sniff it, pointed to the general area and said, "Fetch." He did. Another time he retrieved a wounded otter.

During these years I acquired a piece of property with a small marsh. In Septembers, my boys, the dog, and I would get in the canoe, hide in the cattails, and watch the ducks come in to roost.

The dog's eyes burned with concentration, but he seemed to understand we were only watching. In Octobers we returned on more deliberate missions.

And then, years later, in a log house on a hillside in northern Vermont, he was a black lump in the middle of the living room rug: a tired, groaning, nearly blind, helpless old dog.

One day I noticed a large lump below his right ear. The vet said it was an abscess, and started pumping antibiotics into him. But the dog was old and arthritic, already getting aspirin rolled in hamburger. The antibiotics did not control the abscess and, as I looked at him trying to find a comfortable position in which to sleep, I saw pus oozing from his nose and knew it was time for him to go. I gathered him up, groaning in my arms, and put him in the van. I drove the fifteen miles to the vet's, having called ahead with the news and my decision.

The office was in an old white clapboard house with a wheel-chair ramp leading to the entrance. I parked in what was once the front yard—now a parking lot—lifted the groaning bundle into my arms, and walked up the ramp.

At the top, in front of the office door, I stopped. This was wrong. What I was about to do did not fit my relationship with the animal in my arms. The thought came to me in a swirl—a rush—not really as a logical conclusion, but more like a wave crashing on me. I turned, walked back down the ramp, put my bundle into the van, and drove home. I carried him back up the muddy April path to the house and gently laid him in the middle of the rug.

For the next two days he slept there, interrupted only by my carrying him outside to let him relieve himself.

On the third day the swelling was much worse and, as his head lay across his front feet, the pus again dripped from his nostrils. I sat and stared at an animal who had given me so much pleasure and frustration—an animal who had been my first child, who had eaten most of my first apartment (including several dog-training books), who had bitten a lawyer and not gotten me sued, who had introduced me to many subtleties of the natural world through his nose, who had made so many difficult retrieves, and who had loved and defended our family and our territory. How could I take him to a stranger, even his veterinarian, and arrange for a needle to be run into his vein? Somehow that seemed so inappropriate, so dishonest, so out of context with his life and his pleasure. His being, as was much of mine, was associated with wild places and sunrises, with shotguns, boots, and hunting coats. How could it be right to terminate his life with a needle from a stranger in a sterilized room full of stainless steel and white? Was that not *my* responsibility? Wouldn't the dog expect that it was my responsibility? Wouldn't he think less of me if I did not meet that obligation?

Three days later I *knew* it was not right. I got up from my chair, walked to my desk, scooped several .22 cartridges from the top drawer, and slipped my rifle from the closet. I put on an old hunting jacket, lifted the dog again, and walked out the back door, through the yard, and down across the meadow to the marsh where, the year we made our transition from Georgia pine

183

trees to Vermont sugar maples, the dog had retrieved three whistlers through a half-inch of ice.

I was breathing hard when I put him down in the grass near the cattails. I sat with him for a while.

It was late April and there was some greening in the marsh—some hope of things to come. I could smell manure being spread at the dairy farm across the way. Ice still lurked in the shadows, but the redwings were back and I could hear immature males making territorial claims they would never hold. The old dog sat there. He heard, smelled, and felt it all. I was in front of him, on the wet earth with the rifle cradled across my legs. I looked at him, and talked to him, and thanked him for being so patient, and loyal, and intense, and protective, and tough, and good-humored, and lovable. I cried as I told him all this. And then, while the redwings screeched, the manure spreader hummed, a pair of black ducks settled in, and a warm south wind sifted across the marsh, I shot my dog.

I sat there touching him. He was dead by my hand, but his pain was gone. I took off the old jacket and wrapped him in it. In its pockets was the sediment of many hunts, plus woodcock, grouse, duck feathers, and yes, even some red clay. It was a shroud.

I buried him there because I wanted him to become one with the marsh. And now, when I go back and see the cattails, and the water lilies, and the redwings and the ducks, I know that he is a part of all of it, and I know he would like that. And I know I was right.

CHAPTER TWENTY

The Problem With Holly
By Tom Huggler

According to my mother, who keeps track of such things, by the time I left home at nineteen, a total of thirty-eight dogs had passed through our family of three boys. Some of the dogs actually hunted. I'm forty-eight now and can only guess at how many four-footed partners have shared a finger-fed portion of my lunches served in duck blinds and on truck tailgates. Some of these charges hunted, too, and all are memorable. Let me tell you about one of them.

The problem with Holly is that she is growing old much too fast and may not make it to grouse hunting camp next October. At night my wife and I pill the yellow Labrador with Ascriptin, and Holly whimpers when I massage her arthritic hips too hard. Her wheezing reminds me of an old switch engine slowly chugging through the woods. Her eyes have developed the smoky, opaque look of a glass marble that is flawed. This, I feared, was cataracts, but according to her vet is merely advancing age—and perfectly normal.

I am the one not normal. At nearly thirteen years of age, Holly is the oldest hunting dog I have ever owned, and I am writing about her now because I do not have any experience here and am reasonably certain I will fumble the words later. Whoever said we should pay our tribute to the living, not the dead, was right, and the truth is, I owe this Labrador more than I can tell you in a few short paragraphs.

Holly cost me seventy-five dollars when I bought her in 1980 from a Mayville, Michigan, breeder. I needed a meat-and-potatoes hunter, a partner to fetch ducks and to rout pheasants from the uncivil places my racing setters either missed or couldn't handle. Training? I spent twenty bucks to enroll Holly in a dog obedience class at the local high school. I admit to being surprised when she took first place, beating out a thousand-dollar golden with the improbable name of Octavius.

Holly has shared kennel space with setters most of her life, and they have all taken advantage of this gentle bear-hug of a Labrador. Puppies whose names I can no longer remember thought she was a hairy medicine ball. One rogue got her pregnant; complications followed the abortion, and I had Holly neutered. Another setter nailed Holly on the forehead. Even though she bit back and won the fight, it is she that carries a little hole between her eyes.

About four years ago, my wife and I brought Holly into our house to live, and she has behaved like the good citizen she always was. I have never owned another dog that did not at least bark at the UPS drivers, but Holly offers a grin and a blockish head to pet. She approves of warm hands. A watchdog she is not.

Holly never messes in the house, does not beg, and knows her boundaries. On the other hand, over the years I have noticed an increasing sense of entitlement in direct proportion to the spread of whiteness across her muzzle. Holly refuses to take her pill unless my wife coats it first with peanut butter. She becomes instantly agitated whenever I pack for a trip, and when I do take her along, she insists on riding in the front seat. If dogs could cry! "Insistence" takes the form of squinting eyes, a pink tongue in your face, the disappointed *whap* of an otterine tail along your leg.

The first time Holly smelled birds was the November day I chose her from the basement litter that was eight weeks old. She looked like one of those furry mitts used for washing cars. After sniffing my Bean boots, freshly worn in pheasant cover, she peed on them with excitement. These are the same boots with the chewed-away finger loops—a reminder that Holly once was a puppy—that I still have, somewhere, and probably always will.

Next year, the first pheasant she flushed caused panic, then embarrassment, and then a determination to put the boot to every ringneck on the continent. The following October she learned how to knock geese flat with nose-guard force. The setters were next. One of Holly's goals in life is to find a setter on point, then slam-dunk the dog and take credit for the flush. I lecture her about this often, but she offers those Oriental eyes, grins, and trembles over her skillful revenge. This trait has grown so bad that I have had to attach a twelve-foot checkcord to Holly and tie her to aspens where she howls in misery until released for the retrieve.

Holly has gone everywhere with me, helping to collect game birds from deserts, mountains, plains, and woods. She has tasted all the native grouse and quails, pheasants from a dozen states, and doves, woodcock, partridge, and most species of waterfowl. In Nevada she blundered into a bobcat trap but escaped injury. Another time in Kansas she narrowly missed the strike of a prairie rattler. I have removed Missouri cockleburs, Oklahoma goatshead pickers, and Michigan porcupine quills from her feet, face, belly, and tail. She has never complained.

Aging is a deceptive process, especially in a yellow Lab whose complexion masks a creeping gray face. I first noticed Holly's advancing age four years ago in the Colorado high country when she flagged behind and I, an out-of-shape flatlander, had to wait. In camp last fall she stole away early from our evening fire and found her bed in my tent. I know her hind legs ached from struggling to pull them over logs all day. I know because she licked my hands while I gently massaged her lower back and hips.

Later in Iowa, for the first time I can remember, she did not bark when I unloaded a setter and left her in the truck. The dog ran wild and I kenneled him. I chose Holly and within five minutes she had flushed a ringneck and delivered it with her patented soft retrieve. It was the kind of performance I have come to expect for a decade now, but only learned to appreciate recently.

On a trail, you would never know Holly has a bowed back and drooping tail because she changes into a fluid blonde predator. She can make herself as slim as a nervous grouse. There is a youthful suppleness along with a determined economy to her movement. Holly hunts only where experience tells her birds might be. She knows exactly when I'll rein her in close, so why waste energy going out too far in the first place?

This fall Holly wants to migrate with woodcock throughout eastern North America. We have been sharing thoughts and plans on the subject for several months. As I write this, Holly lies in a yellow pool at my feet, muscles twitching from woodcock fluttering into her dreams.

I thumb through the calendar past too many pages to October.

CHAPTER TWENTY-ONE

Gypsy
By Jerry Gibbs

A black dog came into our lives a while ago. She was a seal-shiny, big-footed pup, unable from the time she could walk to ignore the call of a nose that promised the best of life's wind-borne mysteries. She was a wanderer. Because of that, we named her Gypsy.

Gypsy was a Labrador retriever. Books and trainers acclaim the versatility of the breed, and versatility was what I thought I needed when I decided it was time to get a dog. Later, I learned not to rely on textbook generalities. And I learned about something else you can't take literally: a dog owner's declaration that the heartache of losing a beloved animal is too much to face again. *No more dogs, not ever*, he might say. Don't believe it. If you love dogs, you won't want to be without one, regardless of what may come. But let me tell you about Gypsy.

I had been a long time without a dog. My wife, Judy, and I had been living in apartments, but when we had a couple of boys we needed a house. To me, the best thing about the increased space was that there was room for a dog. We were barely moved in when we found her.

We built a soft nest in a washtub for carrying the pup home from the breeder, but she easily convinced our six-year-old son, Greg, that other places were better. A knot near the tip of her tail gave it the appearance of a windblown flag. That slightly canted tail beat merrily as she wormed herself from the tub onto Greg's lap. She was asleep in moments.

A dog becomes a physical part of your life immediately. Emotionally, it takes just a little longer. You rarely remember the inconveniences of raising a pup. It's the way you remember kids growing up—the good parts stick. With a dog, it's the funny, crazy times, and the way the animal earns your admiration and respect.

Gypsy was seven weeks old when we got her, and a week later she traveled with us on a camping trip to Cape Hatteras, North Carolina. She was too young for water training; in fact, I had yet to introduce her to any water deeper than her drinking pail. It didn't matter—Gypsy was a born water dog. She bounced down the beach, then looked up and discovered the ocean. With her four feet planted defiantly in the sand, she eyed the wind-lashed surf, barked several times, and waded into the wash. I started her training soon after we returned home.

The intensity and single-mindedness of a retriever bent on capturing a dummy or a bird is special, a beautiful thing. Gypsy was barely able to mouth the smallest training dummy I could find, but she managed with no coaxing. My memory of how she grew into the dummies is like an elapsed-time sequence film. I see her growing from bouncing puppy to sleek retrieving machine, her chest in an airborne arc ending in that explosive, flat-out water entry unique to retrievers. Gypsy had spirit and desire; she needed only refining and control.

As Gypsy's training continued, one thing bothered me. Occasionally she broke from a retrieve to follow some intriguing scent. Other times, she seemed to hit a scent and then turn deaf to return commands. The usual remedies, from checkcords to discipline, seemed to work, but only for a while. Friends experienced in dog training chalked up the dog's weakness either to my inept training or to some flaw in her makeup.

The problem did not appear consistently. Long stretches of perfect behavior tended to make us forget Gypsy's occasional lapses. Besides, she was an inseparable member of our family. There were hilarious times when Judy or I released Gypsy into the midst of our boys' softball games. The dog knew exactly what was going on. She charged into the field, seized the ball, and ran the bases several times before stopping.

Gypsy loved winter. She chased our boys' toboggans and usually leaped aboard just before the sled caromed off a mogul and sent her sailing through the air. She played husky in a harness while towing provisions lashed on a sled to winter camp. But it was water that Gypsy loved most of all; she never allowed the boys to swim in peace. As author James Michener once wrote, a Lab is "a kind of perpetual five-year-old, forever young, forever loving."

None of her breaking and running problems were apparent

during water work. She quickly learned to retrieve among decoys without becoming entangled in their anchor cords. I was amazed at the speed with which she learned to make multiple retrieves, to take a line on hand signals, and even to check on command in the midst of one retrieve and head for another target. On land, though, Gypsy's problem continued to recur periodically.

I began to hear of others whose dogs had similar problems. One fellow from Iowa had spent a considerable sum on professional training in hopes that his high-spirited Lab could be used for hunting pheasants. The trainer had accomplished some things, but made no guarantees. The dog's owner had several good days, but eventually the dog locked on one bird that either was running or had left a scent too strong to resist. The Lab cannonballed through the cornfields out of sight. Although the owner brought him back with the whistle, from then on the dog was totally unreliable as a controlled flusher. I didn't like the sound of any of it and went back to preparing Gypsy for waterfowl hunting.

Gypsy's first birds were big, orange-legged blacks and fat, greenhead mallards from the salt marshes of southern New Jersey. We had some good days, that Gypsy dog and I, and I'll remember every one of them. Sometimes we lay flat on the far edges of marsh, away from other hunters, and waited for the birds to come. Flocks of little green-winged teal flashed in the low sun, making quick course changes as they came in. Bigger ducks would make one pass, then bore in straight. We had skies full of geese—Canadas and snows—to watch, and silly grebes to laugh at as we motored back up the big creek. We savored the raspy cry of a startled great blue heron, and that special kind of tiredness that comes after a day of work that you truly love.

Once, during a rain, I explored a section of marsh where I had never been; a high marsh, with grass taller than my head. Gypsy and I pushed far back, though the going was tough and became tougher. Small potholes pocked the marsh. From time to time, we put up a duck. So intriguing was this country that I forgot the reason for the height of the grasses—tide.

When I realized that water was deepening around my boots, I stepped on a small hummock, made a reconnaissance of our position, and began to worry. We had paralleled the side of the marsh from which the flood tide now came. I could not retrace my steps before the water would become too deep, so I could not cut out of the marsh as I had planned. I had to move inland. I was tired, but there was no choice.

As we moved ahead, the marsh became softer. With each step I sank calf-deep, then knee-deep in muck. Rain came in sheets, smoking across the seemingly endless marsh, obliterating the grassy plain before us. I was as wet from perspiration as I would have been without my waterproof parka.

Ducks flushed from potholes in front of us, almost close enough to touch, but I had no time for them. My breathing was ragged, and I had to will each step. Still the tide pressed from behind. When I knelt a moment to rest, Gypsy must have understood the seriousness of the situation because she walked close to me.

Then, when I faltered, she began to bump me with her solid

seventy-five pounds. At first I was enraged; then I realized what she was doing.

We went on like that for what seemed hours before the footing gradually firmed. Finally, I staggered back to the camper, drank two quarts of water, stripped, and began to dry off. Gypsy curled on her pad, steaming, smelling like wet dog, and looking at me with an expression that seemed to say, "Really, we weren't in all that much trouble." I was exhausted. I lay in my bunk wondering just how much she had contributed to getting me back. Even after all of that, I could not accept the dog's faulty behavior on land.

I persisted in trying to work her in upland covers. At times she worked to perfection, quartering ahead, working fields or woodland edges in classic form; then something would catch her interest and she'd drift away. There was no consistency.

I began working her at heel while walking up birds. She bolted very few times during this training. Unhappily, I realized this might be the only way I could trust her away from water. Not long afterward, we moved to northern Vermont.

Big lakes, freshwater swamps, and potholes promised new waterfowling opportunities. We lived in a cottage on a large lake. A decaying blind stood within an easy walk and from it, Gypsy retrieved her first north-country black duck. Whistlers, buffle-heads, geese, and mergansers used the big water.

During the second year, my son Greg helped me construct a more respectable blind on the far side of the lake. We hauled lumber and drove corner stakes while Gypsy swam from shore to blind, explored the beach, and watched our work. She seemed more content to stay close than I had ever seen her. Maybe it was the newness of it all, maybe something else. Those warm, late-summer days of blind-building and hauling out decoys are some of the finest in my memory.

The grouse cycle started up again in Vermont. During spring, the drummers had thumped like old generators. The broods had come through that sometimes worrisome period, and by autumn we were finding not only singles but groups of young ruffed grouse yet to split up. Back in old, rough highland pastures and abandoned orchards, we flushed more birds than I had seen in a long time. The hunting was impossible to resist.

I made a couple of successful hunts alone, holding Gypsy by command at heel. Grouse hunting was so good that I decided to start Greg on these wonderful birds. One afternoon we hunted near the house that we'd built far back on an old logging road. We walked down the road, then cut into the broken woodland. This was mostly thick cover, and any shooting would be fast. I gave the boy the left-handed position—if the going became too rough or too confusing, he could cut to the roadside to get his bearings. To keep track of each other, we talked or whistled back and forth as we moved ahead.

Gypsy was at a tight heel, anxious for a shot bird and the retrieve. Shortly, two birds exploded in front of Greg. When I asked why he didn't shoot, he said he couldn't believe how fast they went. We laughed and moved ahead. Another bird rocketed off somewhere between us, closer to me, but too far to my left for a safe shot. Greg had dropped a little behind, and as I told him to move up, a bird thundered through the trees off my right shoulder. Evidently it had been sitting in a tree, and it had let me pass as grouse sometimes do. The bird flew toward me, then made a ninety-degree turn going away. I fired once and missed.

As I began lowering the 20-gauge, another grouse burst from the ground in dense cover just ahead and slightly to the right. I wheeled quickly and locked on its low flight. Just as I pulled the trigger, my brain screamed a warning to stop. My peripheral vision had detected a black, blurred shape bolting at the bird, but the message was an instant too late. The shot was on its way before my responses caught up and, though I yanked the barrels up, it was a hopeless attempt to correct what had already happened. I remember the roar of my voice over the sound of the gun, then a scream of pain. The dog wheeled in circles as I ran to her, dropped to my knees and cradled her in my arms. I could see where some of the shot had cut through the top of her back. I tried to console her, tried. . . .

Gypsy had stopped crying by the time Greg reached us. Her breathing was ragged, but she did not cry. Her head was on my arm as she watched me patiently, fully trusting me to make things well again. Through blurred eyes I saw that Greg had moved swiftly; no man could have reacted better in an emergency. Both guns were broken, the shells were shucked, and he asked whether I needed help to carry her out. I sent him to bring his mother with the truck, then worked my arms gently beneath the dog, lifted her, and stumbled to the road.

"She'll be all right, won't she?" Greg pleaded. I had nothing to tell him.

The scene of moments before ran over and over in my mind. Never cured of her tendency to break, Gypsy had bolted while I turned away to fire at the first bird. She must have nearly caught the second bird as it frantically beat through the thick, low cover. She had leaped after the escaping grouse into my line of fire.

"Let's hope no pellet struck the spinal column," the veterinarian said. "If it did—well, she could be paralyzed—or she just might not make it. I won't encourage you, or take away all hope."

While the doctor gave her several injections, she watched me quietly, patiently, and with trust. I put a hand beneath her head. She took one deep breath, then rested. I knew she would not live.

Gypsy died during the night. I buried her near a group of birches on a flat place overlooking the woods, the valley below, and the lake, where the duck blind went unused that season. If there is any kind of justice, I know where she is right now. There is a shore with an endless beach to run, a sky full of ducks, and a kid or two to throw sticks and swim with her. Hie on, Gypsy. There's nothing to stop you now.

CHAPTER TWENTY-TWO

An Ordinary Morning
By Joe Arnette

Winter fog veiled the shadowed pair snugged down into a toss of driftwood logs. Vapor hung on the dawn, worn and gauzy in close, then freshening to a thick cloak out over the water. Moisture beaded on the shoulders of the hunter's parka, on his oily gun barrel, on his Labrador's sleek-black coat. The air was cold—near the raw edge of freezing, where a few degrees would turn the nebulous mist into tangible crystals. Given the season, it appeared an ordinary morning.

The blanketed marsh thought so, too. Within the surround of predawn fog, mallards went about their business, chuckling in whispers one moment, pouring out raucous guffaws the next. The splashes of mergansers punctuated the sound of the river lapping its rock-fringed banks like a dog taking a casual drink.

Invisible wings whistled over the blind, shocking wooden thumps from the Labrador's heavy tail. He whined lightly, focused on the opaque curtain out of which the ducks would appear— suddenly and without warning—as they had done so many times. He was a veteran dog, but still anxious that life was passing him by on the wings of each fog-bound bird.

"Hush now," the hunter said, reaching over the short space between them to touch the Lab's ear. He rubbed its leathery tip with his thumb and forefinger. "Stay quiet." His voice stroked the dog as softly as his fingers. "We haven't missed a thing." The hunter looked at his dog's head; though it was obscure in the anemic half-light, he knew its broadly chiseled detail as well as he knew his own reflection. The head was solid and honest, like the brain it held and the body behind it.

Secretly, the man was pleased that the Lab had not lost his puppyish zeal and free-spirited drive for the hunt during the seven seasons they had been together. He had seen too many dogs, for too many sad reasons, without heart for the work. The Labrador at his side was not one of those dogs. Early on, the retriever had given himself to the man and to waterfowling, and when they came together the dog was at his best. And that best had become as good as the man had ever owned or, likely, would ever own, though he sometimes lost sight of it in the dog's steady, day-after-day performance.

The retriever was what he was bred to be—a working gun dog, nothing more. But then, nothing more was necessary. He had never competed in a field trial nor run in a hunt test. He had never been in demand as a stud, nor had anyone tried to buy him. His performance was workmanlike and reliable, which made it look ordinary. It was not. He was a hunting dog, which is another way of saying that beneath the appearance of the commonplace lay the extraordinary.

The Labrador's head twisted upward as a rush of wings broke the white stillness. Six mallards beat low behind the jumble of driftwood, out of the marshes, pushed down by the fog and seeking the river. They passed the dark lumps that were decoys, then disappeared as though erased by the swipe of a hand. Soft, coercing calls from the hunter tensed the Lab, sent a tremor down his body, and riveted his eyes ahead into the thin hint of breeze. Another set of chuckles and the ducks were there, conjured by the calls, backpedaling, their feet down above the blocks.

The dog's eyes locked on the tumbled drake before it arced to the water, lost in the fog. He stayed on his mark, wide-eyed and rigid, until the hunter spoke his name and said, *Dead*. At these words, an excitement-driven *Yip* launched the dog from the driftwood. Five running leaps and he was in the river, an inky line rulered from the blind to the spot where he had last seen the drake. Then he, too, was absorbed by the fog.

"Good boy," the man said, when the Lab had placed the mallard in his hand. "Good job." He fussed over the dog, telling him as he had so often, that the Lab was the best fellow that ever wore a collar. And the hunter meant it.

The man had long ago come to grips with the little *Yip* that fired a retrieve, and he accepted the dog's tendency on his returns to make for the nearest bank and finish the retrieve on land. Both had become irrelevant. The Lab's marks and lines to downed birds were arrow-true; if he chose to escape the icy water on the way back, that was his affair. The man was his only judge, and he considered it sensible. The dog never dropped a bird, never paused in his delivery. Only when he had placed a retrieved duck in his hunter's hand would he relax, shake, and nose the game he had given up—and given up willingly, without a hint of reluctance.

This astounded the man. Although he had trained the Lab, watched him develop, and made the retriever part of his life— along with quite a few others—he was still amazed by the animal's willingness to go against embedded drives. This dog was steady to shot and to fall, took signals well, and delivered to hand—when the mindless instincts of millennia told him to bark and chase, run like hell after the bird, grab it, and eat it on the spot. That he did none of those things, the man thought, was what made each retrieve a singular and truly incredible event.

The man understood the behavioral theories and hands-on mechanics of training; nevertheless, he remained enchanted by quality dog work with its ritualized choreography of grace and beauty. But in his mind, the difficulty or style of the retrieves was not the most remarkable factor in that piece of the hunting equation called a gun dog. Even at the lowest level of skill, he knew that there was something far from ordinary underlying each cooperative performance. The wonder of Labradors was not in superficial judgments of how well they performed; it was hidden within the dogs, in the depths of what they did willingly, and why they did it at all.

Full dawn, such as it was, kicked in on schedule, and the mist, like a collection of tired night spirits, began to fade beneath the gaining light. Cottony wisps of fog disappeared from above the toss of driftwood logs and unraveled over the river. Shapes hardened and acquired texture. The dark lumps on the water became bobbing decoys, and shadows etched themselves into the hunter and his Lab snugged down on a riverbank. For a time, the air would chill, then slowly yield its grip to a pale sun.

Given the season, it appeared to be an ordinary morning.

EPILOGUE
By Gene Hill

If, as one of our philosophers tells us, "history gives man the ability to act with foresight," then the Labrador ought to have a secure future. Some might still feel a bit uneasy about the popularity growth of the breed, and others might be resentful that the Labrador is enjoying its era of being "everyman's dog." The attitude of privilege in possessions dies hard, but die it must. I can't imagine ever being without one or two Labs, nor do I expect to. I need the comfort and companionship they so willingly and amply provide. I have come to absolutely depend on it.

As I write this, I have two sitting comfortingly close by. One gray-muzzled and cloudy of eye, but ready, however painful it is for her now, to go out to the pond and show you the discipline of a fine retrieve. When her great heart wills it, somehow the body responds—the lines of pride, character, and breeding are deep indeed. The other is just a bit more than a puppy; bright-eyed, powerful, and often uncannily intelligent. She will, no doubt, put some bright and shiny ribbons next to the ones on the wall that are fading.

I wish you and your dogs all the pleasures that I have had—and expect to have—with mine. And may there always be a young one full of promise and dedication to take you to those places of wonderment that only admit the person who is introduced by a Labrador retriever.